No Boundaries

No Boundaries

by Jerry Savelle

No Boundaries

Jerry Savelle Ministries

PO Box 748

Crowley, TX 76036

817.297.3155

TABLE OF CONTENTS

I.

Life Without Boundaries

Have you ever thought about the boundaries in your life? We all have them. We have boundaries around our houses—we call them fences. We have boundaries for our cars—we call them parking places. We have boundaries in our houses—we call them bedrooms. We have boundaries in our marriages, boundaries for our kids, and boundaries in our professional lives. There have been books written on the need for boundaries in our lives. And I agree; some boundaries are needed. I need the fence around my house. I don't want just anybody wondering around on my property or coming into my house. My office is a necessary boundary. It's where I go to work, study and spend time with God. When I'm studying, I don't want just anybody coming in and interrupting me. You see my point. That being said, I believe that we've often been blinded to the boundaries that have enslaved us and kept us from living in the blessings of God.

What is a boundary? It's something that indicates a limit. A boundary could be sickness, lack, depression or even complacency. It's anything that keeps you from living the extraordinary life that God planned for each of us before the foundation of the world. Yet most Christians aren't living that life. For the most part, their lives look just like the lives of people who don't know God. Christians are as in debt as anyone else. Christians are getting divorced at the same rate as the world does. Christians are sick and afflicted with disease. As I travel the world, I'm amazed at how Christians are struggling. Many of God's people are under intense pressure and bound to the world's system. They're trapped and don't see a way out. Satan has erected boundaries in their lives and they don't even know it

The truth is that everyone faces boundaries and limitations at some point in their life. It can become easy to live with them, never realizing that Satan is holding you back. Do you know how to recognize boundaries? Do you know where they originated and how to break free? Do you feel as though everything you've depended on in the past is falling apart? Does everything you've worked your whole life to build seem to be crumbling right before your eyes?

Those are boundaries, demonic structures that the devil has erected to keep you out of your destiny. Too often, rather than tearing them down, Christians have had an escape mentality. They get born again and want out of the world. Circumstances have them so whipped they cry, "Come quickly, Lord Jesus! Get me out of this mess!" But that shouldn't be our prayer. Jesus said, "I pray not that thou shouldest take them out of the world, but that thou shouldest keep them from evil," (John 17:15)

Why does Jesus want us to stay here on earth? To live a limitless life free of boundaries. You do it, in part, by recognizing and rejecting the devil's boundaries.

The Apostle Paul said, "For as long as [there are] envying and jealousy and wrangling and factions among you, are you not unspiritual and of the flesh, behaving yourselves after a human standard and like mere [unchanged] men?" (I Corinthians 3:3, Amplified)

You are no longer mere men.

I looked up the word *mere*. It means to have a boundary. When you allow yourself to fall into the works of the flesh, you're living the ordinary life of mere men, with boundaries. The works of the flesh are a big deal to God because they keep you living an ordinary life. Why risk it?

Mere men have boundaries, but Paul said that you are no longer *mere men*. You shouldn't accept the boundaries you had before you were saved. Those limitations no longer belong to you. Why? You're no longer a *mere man*. I love that. I'm not a mere man and neither are you.

Dying to Live an Extraordinary Life

Romans 6:7 in the Amplified Version says, "For when a man dies, he is freed (loosed, delivered) from [the power of] sin [among men]."

You became a new species of being that has never existed before.

I'm sure that you know when you made Jesus the Lord of your life the Bible says your old man died with Christ. You were crucified with Him, and you were raised together with Him. So when you were born again, you died. The old man died. You're a new creation. The literal Greek could be translated to say *you became a new species of being that has never existed before.* This means that the things which held you back before you were saved have no power over you anymore—unless you give it to them.

Paul said to put on the new man. According to Paul, when a man dies, he is freed, loosed, and delivered, not only from Satan, not only from that old sinful nature, but also from the limitations of natural man.

God has called you to live an extraordinary life.

So if you're not supposed to be living with the boundaries of mere men, you may wonder what type of life you should be living. In the Gospel called Good News, the answer to this question is some of the best news yet. It's also a revelation that few Christians have discovered.

God has called you to live an extraordinary life.

If you don't think that living an extraordinary life is scriptural, think again. There's no limit with God. He isn't confined to our world's system. He even proves in His Word that in the midst of a famine and shortage, He can cause His covenant people to excel and to rise above it.

Don't Go To Egypt

In Genesis 26, there was a famine in the land and God appeared to Isaac, the son of Abraham, and said to him, *"Don't go to Egypt."* Why would God tell him that? Because Egypt represented another worldly source, and God didn't want Isaac to go to any source other than Him during this famine. Likewise, today God wants to prove to you and me that even in a famine He can and will take care of His own.

A famine in Isaac's day was like the bad economy in our day. Believe me, this isn't the first time the world's system has failed. God knows what He's doing so you have to trust Him. In Isaac's day, net worth or material assets were not only measured by gold and silver but also by cattle, sheep, flocks and herds. If there was a famine, then it was going to affect your cattle, sheep, flocks and herds. There was going

to be a decrease in your net worth when your flocks begin
dying off because of the famine.

---

*The word bless literally means to empower to
prosper, empower to succeed, empower to excel, and
empower to increase.*

Empowered to Prosper

Right in the middle of this famine God said, "Fear not, for
I am with thee, and will bless thee" (Genesis 26:24). The
word *bless* literally means to empower to prosper, empower
to succeed, empower to excel, and empower to increase.
One of the primary things that will cause you to not be
limited or bound by the world's system is the blessing of
God on your life. The blessing is an empowerment. The
blessing is something that came on you the day you were
born again. The Bible says that among the righteous there
is favor and the blessing of the Lord is upon His people
(Psalm 5:12). The blessing is an empowerment on your life,
and it's what will produce a house, a car, clothes, or whatever it is that you need and are believing God for.

The blessing is on you. Whether you feel like it or not, it's on you. You may not understand it, but its still there. If you're born again, you have something on you that the rest of the world doesn't have on them. You will go to bed tonight with the blessing on you. You will wake up in the morning with the blessing on you. You will go to your job with the blessing on you. That's what makes you different from the rest of the people you work with everyday. They have their own might, ability, intellect, and resources to depend upon, but you do not have those limitations. You have the blessing. The blessing goes beyond what you can ask, hope, think, or even dream (Galatians 3:14).

You will go to bed tonight with the blessing on you. You will wake up in the morning with the blessing on you.

God gave man the ability to reason and problem solve. When you add the blessing to your natural ability, then you go from ordinary to extraordinary. With the blessing you can go from an entry level position to a manager, from renting an apartment to owning your own home, from sickness to health. It's all included in the blessing, and it's how God intended for you to live.

Better Than Your Dreams

Jesus goes on to say in John 10:10, "I am come that they might have life, and that they might have it more abundantly." The Message Bible says it this way, "I came so that they can have real and eternal life, more and better life than they ever dreamed of."

Jesus came so that you might live a better life than you've ever imagined. Jesus came for you to enjoy your life. He didn't come so you could be depressed, lonely, or under pressure all the time. Those feelings are just Satan trying to manifest in your life. If you're not enjoying life, then step back and see who is in charge. Ask yourself if the Word is dominating your thought life or are the world's philosophies and ideas more prevalent in your everyday thoughts? It's good to know what's going on in the world around us, but don't forget that those are all things that you have been redeemed from. You don't have to live with lack. God didn't put that on you as a limit. Boundaries and limits come from Satan because they keep you from having the abundant life that God has planned for you.

In the Amplified Bible John 10:10 reads, "...that I not only came that you might have life, but enjoy life to the full and until it overflows." So let me ask you: Are you living in the overflow?

Don't Be Ignorant

Why aren't more Christians living in the overflow? Why do most Christians just exist? Why do most Christians just survive or barely get by when Jesus made it very clear that it was His purpose to bring life? Unfortunately, many Christians are ignorant of the Word. Many people think that God isn't concerned with them or their problems. That kind of thinking makes it hard for them to understand that God wants them to live life well so they can influence and affect those around them that don't know Him.

I want you to know that I'm enjoying life. I'm presently living life better than I have ever dreamed or imagined possible. I'm living life right now beyond the wildest dreams I had as a young boy. And as a child of God, you should too. God isn't blessing me because of who I am. He is honoring His covenant with me because I choose to trust Him and take Him at His word. He will honor you the same way if you'll remove the boundaries from your life.

---

*When everybody is screaming,
"These are the worst of times!" they don't have to be
the worst of times for you.*

Boundaries and limitations on your life aren't from God. He never intended you to live a limited life. You are limitless through Christ. God hasn't put boundaries on you. He hasn't placed limitations on you. The only limitations you have are the ones you have accepted yourself. When you get in the Word of God long enough, all of those limitations are going to start falling by the wayside. God is the one who says that you can do all things through Him who strengthens you (Philippians 4:13).

Furthermore, God doesn't need a good economy to prosper you. When everybody is screaming, "These are the worst of times!" they don't have to be the worst of times for you.

Out of This World

"Wait a minute, Brother Jerry," you might say, "those limitations and boundaries are just a part of life. That's the way the world works."

That kind of thinking is a boundary in your life which keeps the blessings of God out of it. It's there because you're not familiar with the Bible. This is important so don't miss it: *You're not of this world!*

In John 17 Jesus prayed to the Father and said:

"I have given and delivered to them Your word (message) and the world has hated them, because they are not of the world [do not belong to the world], *just as I'm not of the world.* I do not ask that You will take them out of the world, but that You will keep and protect them from the evil one. *They are not of the world* (worldly, belonging to the world), [just] as I'm not of the world," (verses 14-16, Amplified, emphasis mine).

Notice that Jesus repeated Himself when He said, "They are not of the world." Anything that Jesus says is important, but when He says something more than once, we need to pay close attention. What does it mean to *not be of this world?* It means that you are no longer marked by the same boundaries that the world is. You don't have to share the same restrictions or limitations in life that the world has. You don't have to be under pressure like the world. You have hope. But how do we begin to break free from those limitations?

When you're not of this world, then you're not bound by the laws of this world's system. For non-believers, if the economy is going down so are they. If sickness comes on them, they're restricted to the world's knowledge and resources. Their success is limited to what the world says they can achieve. As a believer, you're not restricted, confined, or held back by the things that non-believers are. You should be healed, prosperous, and successful every day of your life.

Every time the world screams, "No way! No way!"
you ought to think that there is a way. God's way!

In the Message translation, verse 14 says, "They (his followers) are no more defined by the world than I'm defined by the world." The word *defined* here means *marked by its boundaries*. Whatever boundaries the world has, you and I do not have those same boundaries. The world's restrictions and confinements are not our restrictions and confinements.

The limitations the world faces should not hold you back. Everything the world says is impossible shouldn't be impossible for you. Every time the world screams, *"No way! No way!"* you ought to think that there *is* a way. God's way!

You Can Do It

Anybody reading this book can experience a limitless, boundary-free, extraordinary life. You *can* do it. If I can break the boundaries that were on my life, then so can you. If you're willing to go the extra mile, then you can expect the extraordinary to take place in your life. This is what I consider to be above and beyond: **thinking bigger, dreaming bigger, believing bigger, standing longer, persevering longer and sowing more.** What am I talking about? Bigger than who? Longer than who? More than whom? Bigger, longer, and more than the average Christian. Who wants to be average? Who wants to be mediocre?

Whatever level the average Christian thinks on, the extraordinary person thinks bigger than that. Whatever level the average Christian dreams on, the extraordinary Christian dreams bigger than that. Whatever level the average believer believes at, then the extraordinary believer believes bigger than that. Whatever level of tolerance the average Christian has, the extraordinary Christian's tolerance is greater than that. Whatever level of sowing the average believer sows at, the extraordinary believer sows more. He's willing to go further. He's willing to stand longer. He's willing to persevere longer.

This is the law of cause and effect. You can't ask God for the extraordinary life if you're not willing to do more than the average person. It's been said that the definition of insanity is doing the same thing over and over but expecting different results. That doesn't make any sense. You can't do the same things over and over and expect it to yield different results, but Christians do so every day. They want to live in prosperity, but they don't want to spend any time in the Word or any time in prayer. **You can't expect to experience a change if you don't change something that you're doing.** You have to take it to another level!

My friend, I want to tell you that the boundaries that have kept you enslaved are about to be broken. God has an extraordinary life planned for you, a life without limits, and it's time that you start walking in it! Are you ready for an extraordinary adventure? I believe you are and that's why you're reading this book. I trust that as you apply these principles in your own life, the boundaries that have kept you back will begin to fall away and you will soon be living the life that you, and God, have dreamed of. Get ready—God has given me an exciting, life-changing, boundary-breaking word for *you!*

II.

Breaking Through

There was a time when the boundaries in my life squeezed so tight that they felt like a noose around my neck. I was failing at everything. My business was failing. My marriage was failing. My finances were failing. I was so tired of failure that I couldn't take it any more. I knew that if I didn't get the limitations out of my life, I would never succeed.

I was sick like the world. I was broke like the world. I was depressed like the world. My life was ordinary and I had no hope of anything better because I was confined to the world's way of thinking. I grew weary of just existing. I grew tired of religion and developed a hunger for God.

When my desperation for change reached its peak, I closed my paint and body shop and went into in a little spare bedroom with the Bible. For the next three months I spent hours each day reading and studying the Word of God. I treated my time learning the Word like it was a full time job. The Word was *that* vital to me. I knew it was the difference between success and failure in my life. During that time, I realized that God wasn't the one limiting me. The real shocker came when I discovered that the primary culprit in my own life was *me*. The longer I delved into the Word of God, the more I realized that not only had the Lord *not* put restrictions and limitations on me, He'd gone to the cross to remove the very ones I was tolerating. I discovered that my failure was a product of how I'd been raised and the habits I'd formed since. My own words, thoughts and behavior patterns were keeping me from being a winner.

Now you've got to understand that at this point nothing had changed in the natural. After I finished praying and studying the Word, I had the same debts. My life was still a dismal downward spiral of failure. But everything was changing on the inside of me. *I* was changing from the inside out. My thoughts were being renewed. My heart was being renewed. On the inside, everything that made me Jerry Savelle was changing because I was being renewed by the Word of God.

You have to change on the inside before anything will ever change on the outside. But once you begin to change on the inside, it won't be long before you'll be able to see changes on the outside. The more the Word grew on the inside of me, the more perfected the image of winning and becoming an overcomer grew and the more I saw outward manifestations of that inward change.

Criticism

And when you begin to break through those boundaries, when your bank account has extra money in it, when you get promotion after promotion, when your marriage becomes all that you have dreamed it could be, let me forewarn you that people, even some Christians, might be critical of you. If they are, don't worry about it. It's just their carnal-minded way of saying, "I wish I were you." When somebody is critical of me, I just walk away thinking, *They wish they were me.* Now you might think that sounds arrogant, but it's not. It's knowing who you are in Jesus and whom you serve. So don't sweat it when people become critical of you, know that you are experiencing the life that God has always planned for you and just keep walking in it.

*You have to change on the inside before
anything will ever change on the outside.*

Fire In My Eyes

At the end of those three months, I came out of that
bedroom a new man. I had the fire of God in my eyes, the
Word of God in my heart and the power of God in my
hands. The favor of God manifested in my life every day.
God's blessings followed me wherever I went.

When I dove into the depths of the Word of God, I discovered that I wasn't defined by this world. That's when
I started breaking loose from the world's system. Now, it
didn't happen in a week. It didn't happen in a month. But
radical changes were occurring in my life. I'll be honest,
people thought I was crazy. However, it didn't take long before those same people were calling me when they needed
help.

I still remember the way it felt when the boundaries in my
life tightened into a noose. However, I have a more vivid

memory of the day Carolyn and I walked into a car dealership and paid cash for a new car. Another hall-of-fame memory was the day we finally lived in a debt-free house. We'd broken through the boundary of lack in our lives! The day we paid cash for a car for someone else is a day that's forever freeze-framed in my memory. The world can't even fathom doing these things, but without boundaries, they should be everyday occurrences for believers.

If I'd known that life could be this good when I was younger, I wouldn't have waited so long to make Jesus the Lord of my life. Religion lied to me. All I ever heard growing up was, "God's going to get you!" That's just ridiculous. Don't you think that if God wanted to get you, you'd already be got? Who can outrun God?

At the end of those three months, I came out of that bedroom a new man. I had the fire of God in my eyes, the Word of God in my heart and the power of God in my hands.

I broke through the fences Satan had erected in my life. I broke through the boundaries the world called normal and

learned to live an extraordinary life. As wonderful as that
is, let me give you the sobering news. I wasn't the only one
who heard the messages that drove me to the Word. Hun-
dreds of other people heard the same Word, but they didn't
apply it. Everyone who heard that Word could have dove
into the Bible for themselves and come out changed. They
heard the Word but they didn't act on it and apply it. Those
people had the same opportunity that I had, but they chose
to go on living within the world's boundaries.

You've come to a crossroads in your life. Within the pages
of this book I'm going to teach you the things you need to
know to break through the boundaries in your life. Whatever you do, don't finish the last page of this book, close it
and go on with life as usual.

Knowing these principles is crucial in breaking through the
boundaries in your life. But if you don't apply them, nothing will change. When you apply them, you'll break free
from the boundaries of poverty, sickness and every form of
defeat and failure. The Word of God will separate you into
a higher form of reality than the world knows.

was hunger for God that drove me past all the boundaries in my life, and I've never been hungrier and thirstier for Him than I am today. *"Blessed are those who hunger and thirst for righteousness, for they will be filled"* (Matthew 5:6 NIV).

The Word is the only thing that can break the boundaries and limits in your life.

The First Step

You might be asking, "Okay, Brother Jerry, how do I get rid of these limitations and break those boundaries? I've heard those things all my life. I just thought that's the way it was." The answer is the Word of God.

The most important first step in breaking through your boundaries is letting the Word of God change you from the inside out. You must discover who you are in the Word of God, what you can do through the Word of God, and for you to *really* understand that you have a covenant with Almighty God. Once you do that, your life will forever be changed—just like mine was. I want you to know that

Amen

something is going to happen on the inside of you. And let me tell you, it's the beginning of the end for the boundaries and limits that have held you captive.

You might be thinking, "Are you sure?"

Yes, I am. And do you know why? Because God has promised in His Word that no weapon formed against *you* shall prosper (Isaiah 54:17). That means that you should come through every trial on top—not below, not beneath, and not just barely breathing. You can be more than a conqueror – because that is what God says you are (Romans 8:37). He says that you are more than a conqueror *through Jesus*!

Do you understanding what I am telling you? God plans for you to come out victorious no matter what your situation. He already has your victory planned. When you understand this, a revolution will take place in your life.

When Jesus was about to go to the cross, He didn't want to leave until He knew His disciples understood the importance of the Word. In John, chapter 17, He said, "I have given them thy word," (v. 14). In the mind of Jesus the most important thing that He could leave with His followers was the Word of God.

In the world today it's easy to take the Word for granted. We have such easy access to it. You can buy a Bible at just about any bookstore. You can download it as an app on your Iphone. You can upload one to your computer. We have the Bible on CDs. You can buy sermons online. You have *access* to the Word like never before. But do you *apply it* to your life?

You have access to the Word like never before. But do you apply it to your life?

The Word was so important to Jesus that before He finished His mission, He was able to say to His Father, "If there is one thing I have done, I have given them Your word."

Why was it so important that Jesus let His Father know that He had given the disciples His word? Because **the Word, and the power of the Word, is what separates you from the world**. "I have given them thy word; and the world hath hated them, because they are not of the world, even as I am not of the world." Jesus' followers were no more of this world than He was. Are you a follower of Jesus today? If so, He was talking about you just as much as He was talking about His original followers.

I'm *in* the world, but I'm not *of* it, and neither are you. That's what makes the difference. If you're still of it, then you've got problems.

> *Your first thought in a trial should be what does the Word say about this—not what does the world say.*

If you're still trying to hang onto some of your past or things that are worldly, you won't be victorious. Everyone faces trials, but you shouldn't react like normal people do. *You're not normal.* You're not supposed to react like everyone else. You shouldn't think like them. You shouldn't talk like them. You shouldn't act like them. You shouldn't live like them.

Your first thought in a trial should be what does the *Word* say about this—not what does the *world* say. You're not restricted or confined by the same things they are because you are not ordinary like the world.

It's Your Nature

The Bible says in 1 John 5:4 that you are born of God. That means you possess His nature. Is God a normal god? No. He's an extraordinary God. There's nothing average about God. That's the reason He is referred to as Most High. No other god can come close to Him. That's the reason He asks, "Is there any God like me?" He's an extraordinary God! There is nothing ordinary or average about Him. Everything He does is extraordinary.

Set Apart

John 17:17 says, *"Sanctify them through thy truth: thy word is truth."*

The word *sanctify* simply means to set apart or to separate. This is how we should function in the world today—set apart. But the key to living life set apart from the world is to *know the Word.* The reason so many Christians are failing today is because they don't truly know the Word. Don't get me wrong, it may be in their *head*, but it's not in their *heart*. *Key*

Why? Because they haven't put a strong enough empha-sis on the importance of God's Word. Reading your Bible once a week is not enough. You'll never be extraordinary until you place as much importance on the Word as you do your next meal. Hunger after the Word, and it will change you. Make it a priority over your favorite television show and see what God will do for you. Knowing the Word is the only way to be the overcomer that God has called you to be.

> *The reason so many Christians are failing today is because they don't truly know the Word.*

God separates you from what's going on in this world through the Word. If you don't know the Word, you'll be in the same boat as the rest of the world. When the flu comes around, you'll get it. When they are laying off people at your job, you will start packing. But that isn't how God intended for you to live.

Who You Associate With

I believe that one of the biggest boundaries in many Christians lives is their friends. They're running with the wrong people. Instead of being an influence on non-believers, they just act like the people they hang around. God never intended for you to be like non-believers. He intended for you to be different and cause them to want to be like you.

Wow

That means you can't be normal. Your life has to be set apart. It has to be different. For your friends to want to be like you, then you have to live in the supernatural. You have to live extraordinary, not ordinary like they are. And it's God's Word that will take you out of the norm and take you into the extraordinary. You can be off limits to the devil if you know who you are in the Word. He may try to attack you, but he'll never win.

The Real Truth

The last part of John 17:17 says, "...thy word is truth." The word *truth* is defined *as the highest form of reality that exists*. This means that there are other forms of reality, but God's Word is *the* highest form of reality.

The world is just reporting what they see happening out there. It's factual. It's real, but it's not the *highest* form of reality. The highest form of reality is the Word of God. God's Word doesn't make any sense to the natural, carnal mind. But since it is the highest form of reality that exists, and every other word is a lower form of reality, then the lower form must bow to the higher form. The lower form of reality has to bow to the Word every time. *Amen.*

The doctor may say your have terminal cancer. That may be true based on his information, but there is a higher form of reality. The highest form of reality says, "...*by whose stripes you were healed,*" (1 Peter 2:24). Cancer has to bow to Word, and the Word says that you were healed by the stripes that Jesus bore for you! Who do you choose to believe? The Word, or the doctor? I choose the Word every time.

I am *word* oriented, not *religious tradition* oriented. Religious tradition says, "You never know what God will do." Or, "God gave you that sickness to teach you something." No. That is not true. God will not go against His Word.

You can't look at your sickness and say, "This is how God wants me to be." That doesn't line up with His word. The Word must be first place and final authority in your life. You don't have to allow what's happening in the world to happen to you, because you are not limited to what the world is limited to. You are set apart—because of the Word. _Jesus_

I pray that this truth and the importance of the Word becomes a revelation to you. When it does, nothing can stop you from being extraordinary. It won't matter what's going on in the world because you will be able to maintain your joy, your focus, and your faith. You'll know that God is going to come through for you—no matter what the world, or your circumstances say. When this becomes a revelation to you, it will forever change you. You'll be confident because you'll know that God will see you through because it's His word that separates you from all the other junk that's going on out there.

All the Wrong Places

Your problems may be so big that you think, *"Maybe the government can help me. They owe me. I deserve a little bit of help."* Let me tell you, if you're looking to the government for answers or to pay your bills, you're in trouble. They don't have the answers. The Word does. Get in the Word for yourself. You can't be lazy and extraordinary at the same time. The answer to your situation is in the Word, find out what it says and dare to believe it. If you're willing to do that then you will soon discover that God will back it every time.

You don't just hope that you can go from ordinary to extraordinary. You have to live it on purpose.

You don't just hope that you can go from ordinary to extraordinary. You have to live it on purpose. This is deliberate. God set it up that way. He put the ball in your court. God sees you blessed, highly favored, and living life better than you ever imagined. That is His plan for you. Do you see it that way? Are you committed to living that life? If so, then the Word has to be final authority in your life.

The Bible tells us in Proverbs 15:30, "Good news nourishes the bones," (Amplified). The Word will build you up, maintain you, and support you when everything else fails. When I walk away from my time in the Word, I feel good. I'm encouraged. I feel like I could take on the world. I have an assurance that God is about to do something good. When I walk away from the Word, I know I can live the extraordinary life. And God is no respecter of persons. If I can do this, so can you. Remove the limitations in your mind and replace them with a promise in the Word.

Attitude Determines Altitude

When things are changing on the inside of you, it will have an affect on your attitude as well. Instead of being negative about everything, you'll catch yourself becoming positive. While everybody else is talking negative, all of a sudden, something positive will be coming out of your mouth. Changing inwardly will affect your attitude and your actions. You may even get to the place where you don't want to be around some of the same people because of their negativity. That's when you know it is working. That's when you know what you're doing is finally paying off. When you don't talk like the world, when you don't think like the world, and when you don't have their attitude anymore that's when you know this transformation is taking place.

If you want to take the limits off of your life, you're going to have to do more than is required, go the extra mile, and exceed what others might be willing to do.

The only way you can change what's in your heart is to reprogram it with the Word of God. You have to get the Word of God in your heart in *abundance*. That doesn't mean you need to quit your job and spend three months in a bedroom like I did. However, it's mandatory that you give the Word the highest priority. When the Word is in your heart in abundance, it won't matter what's going on around you because the Word that's in you will come out and affect your circumstances. That's what will keep you from being restricted with the world's restrictions.

Bottom Line

If you want to take the limits off of your life, you're going to have to do more than is required, go the extra mile, and exceed what others might be willing to do. That's how you experience the extraordinary life. What's the principle here? If you want to live this kind of life, you've got to be willing to do what ordinary people are not willing to do. What do I mean by that? You have to do more than is required. You might be thinking, "How much time do I have to spend in the Word every day? How much time do I need to pray? How much do I need to sow?" Let me answer those questions with one of my own.

Do you want a mediocre life or do you want the extraordinary?

The extraordinary person doesn't look for just what is required. They're willing to do more than is required. They're willing to go the extra mile. They're willing to exceed what others are willing to do. As a result, they have put into motion the law of cause and effect. Their action is about to produce for them an equal reaction. If you become extraordinary in the way you approach the Word, your walk with God, and your Christianity, then you will be rewarded with the extraordinary instead of the ordinary.

III.

PRESS!

Once you get the Word of God inside of you and discover who you are, then the fight is on. And let me tell you, it's a fight. The devil isn't going to sit by quietly and just let you break through the boundaries that he has worked so hard to place around you. He doesn't want you living an unlimited life. He doesn't want you actually living the life God has planned for you. He understands that knowing about it and living it are two different things. He doesn't mind you *knowing* that God has a great life planned for you, he just doesn't want you to *live* it. Why? Because then you become a threat to him. When you break through the boundaries and barriers in your life, you can help others break through theirs. He doesn't want that. So believe me, it will be a fight. But it's a fight that you *can and will* win if you won't give up and if you'll refuse to quit.

Once I saw in the Word what God wanted me to have, the fight was on. The devil didn't say, "Oh, he heard the truth. Everybody back off. We can't attack him now." No. Once you hear the truth, alarms go off in Satan's domain. *He heard the truth—attack!*

*You must make standing against the devil a part of
your life. Every time he attacks, you attack him!*

The fight is on, and this is where pressing comes in. Pressing is what separates the men from the boys. In Philippians 3:14 Paul said, *"I press toward the mark."* It's a little phrase but I promise you it's the difference between success and failure. That phrase carries a lot of weight.

Boundaries are not going to just fall off of you. You have to engage in a battle to be loosed from them. You must make standing against the devil a part of your life. Every time he attacks, *you attack him!* Do like David, the shepherd boy, did when he fought Goliath. Run to the battle lines and attack! Meet him on the front and push him back where he belongs, which is under your feet!

I've made pressing a part of my nature. I can't imagine why any child of God would ever, under any circumstance, give up. God has given us His Word with all of His promises in it, why would you quit?

We win!

Jesus won the battle and the devil is under our feet.

Fight Back

The Apostle Paul saw what God wanted for him. He saw in the spirit what was ahead, but it didn't become a reality until he was willing to *press*. You must press for the extraordinary life. Are you willing to press for it? I've noticed that people who win are the ones who press.

The devil may get in your face in the middle of the night and say, "There's no way out for you. You'll never get the amount of money you need. Your body will never be healed. Your marriage will never be restored. Your kids will never be delivered from drug addiction."

> *"If it's a fight you want, it's a fight you're going to get. When the dust settles, God and I will win!"*

When he does, you just tell him, "If it's a fight you want, it's a fight you're going to get. When the dust settles, God and I will win!" Break that barrier through the Word of God!

What battle would you not fight if you knew that defeat wasn't an option?

God doesn't create losers. He doesn't know how to lose. In the mind of God there are only winners and mighty achievers in His family. You have the capacity and the God-given ability through the Word of God to break every barrier that Satan says cannot be broken. When Satan says, "No!" God says, "Yes!"

"Well Brother Jerry," someone said, "how do I fight the devil?"

The same way Jesus did. He said, "It is written…" Remember all that Word you've put in your heart? Loose it like a slingshot out of your mouth at the devil!

The Battleground of the Mind

The biggest battle you're going to have to fight is the battle for your mind. Why? It's because limitations and boundaries take root in the mind. There's nothing you'll ever do that isn't born first as a thought.

Are you ready for your life to be transformed from ordinary to extraordinary? Let me show you how that happens. Romans 12:2 says, *"And be not conformed to this world, but be ye transformed by the renewing of your mind."*

The Phillips translation of that verse says, "Don't let this world around you squeeze you into its mold." Paul said that to eliminate the world's boundaries away from your life, you must renew your mind. And it's not something that you can do once. It's something that you're going to be doing for the rest of your life.

I've been working on this since I was born again. I didn't wake up one day and say, "Okay, I'm done. My mind is renewed." As long as you're on this planet you're going to have to be renewing your mind. It's something you do every day. If you stay out of the Word for a few weeks, just watch what will happen. You'll start picking up on what the world is saying and doing. The next thing you know, things will start coming through your mind and out your mouth that you once had control over. Limitations and boundaries begin in the mind, so be selective about what you think.

It's imperative that you change the way you think. And I can tell you from experience that this doesn't happen overnight. No wonder God told Joshua to meditate the Word by day and by night (Joshua 1:8). I think an interesting parallel in the Old Testament is when God supplied manna for His people in the wilderness. Have you ever noticed that they had to go gather it everyday? They couldn't just gather a heap that would last them for the year. No, they had to go get fresh manna every day. It's the same with you and me. Renewing our minds must be a daily activity. When the Israelites gathered more manna than enough for one day, it spoiled. God wanted them to gather it up everyday. We too must be in the Word everyday.

Fresh Manna

You need fresh manna daily. The Word of God is your manna, and you need it every day of your life. Once again, if you stay out of the Word for a couple of weeks and start listening to the media all the time then, you'll catch yourself saying the things that the world says and accepting the limitations that they have. Renewing your mind is a continual process, but it's what separates you from the rest of the world. The extraordinary kind of life requires you to change the way you think.

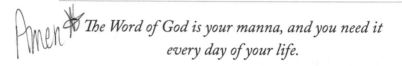

The Word of God is your manna, and you need it every day of your life.

Amen

The Real You

The Bible tells us in Proverbs 23:7, *"For as a man thinketh in his heart, so is he."* The way you think in your heart is the real you. You may put on a façade for people, but it can't fool God. He knows how you really are by what's in your heart. How you see yourself on the inside is how it's going to be on the outside. Once again, the extraordinary has to take place on the inside before it can ever take place on the outside. If you can't see yourself driving that new car, you'll never receive it. If you can't see yourself healed, you'll always be sick. If you can't see yourself prosperous, you'll always be in lack. You have to be able to conceive it in your heart.

Mirror, Mirror

2 Corinthians 3:18 in the Amplified Bible says, *"And all of us, as with unveiled face, [because we] continued to behold [in the Word of God] as in a mirror the glory of the Lord, are constantly being transfigured into His very own image in ever increasing splendor and from one degree of glory to another."* This means that God's Word is like a mirror. When you look in a mirror, you see a reflection of yourself. The Word is a mirror, and the reflection that you'll see in this mirror is not the way your parents saw you, nor the way the world sees you, and not even the way carnal-minded Christians see you. Instead, you are going to see a reflection of the way God sees you. You'll never go to God's Word and look in this mirror and see yourself poor, depressed, sick, or hopeless. That's not the reflection, or the image that the Word of God will paint on the inside of you. If you're not looking in the Word, then you have a distorted image of yourself.

*You'll never go to God's Word and
look in this mirror and see yourself
poor, depressed, sick, or hopeless.*

It's a lot like the fun room with the distorted mirrors at the carnival. Imagine standing there and looking into these mirrors. You might look really tall and skinny or really short and wide. If you're looking into any other mirror outside of the Word of God, then you're going to get a distorted image of yourself and not the image that God sees. However, if you continue to look in the mirror of the Word, then you'll be transformed into His image from one degree of glory to another. That means you'll keep going higher. You'll keep going from one level to another until you reach the extraordinary life.

*When others quit pressing, I kept pressing.
When others gave up, I didn't.*

It's Up to You

Obviously, you have a part to play in this. God's not going to make all this happen just because you decided to get saved. That's the starting point, but then you have to get in the Word and continue in it day and night. That's what I did. I continued in it. When others quit pressing, I kept pressing. When others gave up, I didn't. When others said, "It doesn't work," I turned a deaf ear to those words and said, "That may be what you believe, but I don't believe that. It's working for me." Sometimes you have to get to the place that when people are talking negative and saying it doesn't work, you just put a smile on your face, look them straight in the eye, and never hear a word they say.

The more time you spend in the mirror of God's Word, then the more you'll become what you see. Remember, it has to happen on the inside before it can happen on the outside. Can you see yourself living an extraordinary life or do you see yourself being ordinary? Can you see yourself going further than anybody in your family has ever gone? If your family has never been able to pay cash for anything, do you see yourself being able to pay cash? If everyone in your family has been in debt and lived on borrowed money, can you see yourself being the first one to break the mold? If you can't see that on the inside, then there's no chance of it ever happening on the outside. All you need is to spend more time in the Word.

The more time you spend in the mirror of God's Word, then the more you'll become what you see.

Catch the Vision

By now, you know that God wants you to be free from an ordinary, average life and wants you to live an extraordinary kind of life. It's your decision whether it actually happens. God wants it for you, but the question is this: How badly do you want it?

If you're committed to living an extraordinary life, a life without boundaries, then, once again, you have to have a vision of the extraordinary life on the inside of you. You have to have a picture on the inside of you of what living that kind of life would be like.

One of the definitions of vision is a mental image. Obviously, this is referring to seeing something on the inside. Have you heard the phrase, "I saw it with my mind's eye"? This phrase refers to seeing something on the inside before it can be seen on the outside. Can you see yourself living beyond the norm? Can you see yourself living beyond average or are you stuck with the limitations that everyone else has?

Vision is really insight into the plan, the will, and the purpose of God for your life. Psalm 119:130 says, "The entrance of thy words giveth light." It's only through the Word that you're able to see in your mind and in your heart what God's plan is for your life. Without the Word, the vision will never come to pass. The more Word you put in you, the more light that's shined on your vision and it becomes clearer what God has planned for you. The clearer your vision is, the more determined you'll be to stand strong until it becomes a reality.

To Help Others

Why does God want you to live a life without limits? To help others. The real reason Jesus came to give abundant life wasn't so you can hoard it up on yourself, but so you can become a distribution center to the families of the earth.

God blesses you so you can bless others. God is not trying to keep things from you. He is trying to get things to you. He wants you to come out of the mindset you were brought up in of poverty, sickness, defeat, depression, or loneliness and get the Word into your heart and break those boundaries—so you can help others do the same

You might be a person with a good job and living a good life. These could be the best times you have ever seen, but that does not mean that you can't experience more. You need to keep stirring yourself up and pushing toward the next level. Don't allow yourself to become complacent. Keep reaching for everything God has in store for you.

He has bigger plans for your life. He wants you to live an extraordinary life in a world that is ordinary. Ordinary people go with the flow, extraordinary people strive for more. They say, "I'm not staying in this place forever. I am getting up and moving on no matter what is going on around me."

Don't Settle for Less

It's amazing to me how some people are willing to settle for less than God has planned for their lives even after they learn they don't have to. They've heard that they don't have to be ordinary. They've heard that they don't have to have the same limits on them that the world does, but they're still willing to settle for less than God's best. Then they come up with excuses as to why it can't happen to them. As far as I am concerned, an excuse just means that you're willing to settle for less than God's best for your life.

Have you ever turned on your television and seen a commercial about how you can get out of debt? Sure you have. We all have. You watch it and get inspired, but then you start making excuses about why being debt free can't happen for you. What you're really saying is, "I'm willing to settle for less."

An excuse just means that you're willing to settle for less than God's best for your life.

Provision Has Been Made

The story of the prodigal son is found in Luke 15:

"Then He said: 'A certain man had two sons. And the younger of them said to his father, 'Father, give me the portion of goods that falls to me.' So he divided to them his livelihood. And not many days after, the younger son gathered all together, journeyed to a far country, and there wasted his possessions with prodigal living. But when he had spent all, there arose a severe famine in that land, and he began to be in want," (verses 11-14).

In other words, there was a recession and times were hard. They were living during a time of bad economy. The next two verses go on to say, "Then he went and joined himself to a citizen of that country, and he sent him into his fields to feed swine. And he would gladly have filled his stomach with the pods that the swine ate, and no one gave him anything."

Have you ever been so low you would do something that you'd normally never consider? That's what this son did. He was so desperate and hungry that he was willing to eat what the swine were eating. When he came to himself he thought, *"Wait a minute. My father's servants have more than enough food!"*

He remembered that everyone living at his father's house enjoyed an abundant life. They had food to spare. Back at his father's house, there was an extraordinary and unlimited lifestyle. He came to himself, but not entirely. He came to himself in that he remembered that in his father's house people lived the abundant and extraordinary life and not the ordinary kind of life. However, he was so down on himself for what he had done that he was willing to settle for less than what his father had in store for him.

In verses 18 and 19 he said, "I will arise and go to my father and will say to him, 'Father, I have sinned against heaven and before you, and I am no longer worthy to be called your son. Make me like one of your hired servants.'"

He was saying that he knew in his father's house there was an abundant lifestyle, but that he was no longer worthy of it. He knew he had sinned. He knew he had blown it. He knew that he had messed up royally.

He was willing to go back and be treated like a servant rather than a son. Did you notice what he said? He knew what was available, but he was willing to settle for less. The son didn't truly understand how much his father loved him, and he didn't comprehend the power of forgiveness. It's commendable that he knew he'd messed up and he was sorry for it, but he wanted to start over like a servant—not a son.

However, when his father saw him coming, he told everybody to get the fatted calf ready, get the robe ready, and get the ring ready, because his son was on his way back home.

God's Plan for you Hasn't Changed

Even though his son had messed up and didn't deserve an extraordinary life, the father's plan for his life had never changed. Listen, I don't care what you've done, I don't care what kind of sin you've been involved in, and I don't care how you've royally messed up your life, once you repent, don't come crawling back to God saying, "I'm so unworthy. I don't deserve this unlimited lifestyle. Just let me have the crumbs."

God doesn't want that for you. In your Father's mind, you have just as much right to the extraordinary and the uncommon life now as you did before you ever messed up.

Receive your forgiveness and then go ahead and live the extraordinary life that God says belongs to you.

IV.

THE BIGGEST BOUNDARY

In order to break through the boundaries in your life, you're going to have to settle, once and for all, what you truly believe about the nature of God. Do you really believe that He wants you to live an extraordinary life? Do you truly believe that He loves you that much?

If you've accepted boundaries and limitations on your life, they're not from God. The devil has duped you into settling for something that isn't what God wants for you. In the same verse where Jesus said that He came to provide for you abundant life, He also described Satan's plan for your life. In another place, Jesus said that Satan is the father of lies and that there is no truth in him. *"He was a murderer from the beginning, and abode not in the truth, because there is no truth in him. When he speaketh a lie, he speaketh of his own: for he is a liar, and the father of it,"* (John 8: 44).

In the Garden of Eden, God told Adam and Eve not to eat from one particular tree or they would die. The devil told Eve, *"You shall not surely die,"* (Genesis 3:4).

He called God a liar then, and his tactics have never changed.

He convinced Eve that God didn't have her best interests at heart. The sad truth is that the majority of people—even Christians—are buying that same lie. Satan will always try to convince you that God is out to get you, but nothing could be farther from the truth.

Jesus cleared it up in John 10:10 when He said, *"The thief cometh not, but for to steal, and to kill, and to destroy: I am come that they might have life, and that they might have it more abundantly."*

I've said it before, but it bears repeating. Satan has one thing on his mind: to steal, kill and destroy. But in the process, he wants to deceive you into thinking that those things are coming from God.

The Nature of God

The biggest boundary you must remove is the one that questions the nature of God. As you delve into the Word, you'll see that the Scriptures reveal His nature. God is good. God is faithful. God is love. God is forgiving. God is gracious. God is patient. God is kind. God is long-suffering. God is just.

Who'd want to serve a God who puts sickness on people or intentionally hurts them?

That's why I cringe when someone says, "God put this sickness on me to teach me a lesson," or "I didn't get that raise because God was mad at me." When I hear statements like that I think, *They don't know Him.*

Who'd want to serve a God who puts sickness on people or intentionally hurts them? I can't believe that anyone could think that about God. What kind of parent would do that to their child? Let me tell you, it has never once, even on my worst day, entered my mind to strike my children with some sort of terminal disease, or any disease for that matter. I've never, not a day in their lives, wished them harm. Not even when I was disappointed in them. Yet people actually believe that God made them sick, or struck their house with a tornado or caused a car wreck. Those were all plots and schemes of the devil that have been attributed to God.

The problem with these kinds of statements is that they project a negative image of God in the minds of people which in turn causes them to think that God doesn't care about them. And nothing could be further from the truth. God cares for you. He loves you. He wants His best for you! He doesn't want a life of poverty for you. He doesn't want sickness to be the norm for you. He doesn't want you bound or limited by anything. As a matter of fact, as you study the Word closely, it will become obvious to you that God is not the author of the limitations in your life. He is not the one causing things to go wrong in your life.

God is Faithful

I can't say that God has always showed up in my time frame, but I can tell you that He has always shown up. He has never let me down. I took Him at His Word. He said to prove Him and see if He wouldn't do what He promised. And He always has. If there is one thing I can say about God it's that He's faithful. God says in His Word

73

that He will not break His covenant nor alter the thing that has come from His lips (Psalm 89:34), so take Him at His Word. He will come through for you.

Surprise!

God isn't out to get you. He wants to help you. He came that you and I might have life and that we might have it more abundantly. God wants His children to enjoy life to the fullest. There shouldn't be any other person's life which you envy. People should be envious of your life. If they're not, then get into the Word, breakthrough the boundaries and limits on your life, and change your ordinary life into an extraordinary one.

God wants to surprise you with blessings everywhere you go. God is constantly looking for ways to bless you.

Deuteronomy 28:2 says, *"And all these blessings shall come on thee, and overtake thee if thou shalt harken to the voice of the Lord thy God."* One of the meanings of the word *overtake* is surprise. God wants to surprise you with blessings everywhere you go. God is constantly looking for ways to bless you. He wants to bring you joy. Yet we constantly tie His hands.

Created to be Different

How do we tie God's hands? By talking just like the rest of the world is talking. By acting just like the rest of the world is acting. By being depressed and discouraged like the rest of the world, and accepting the same limitations. God never intended for us to be like them. He created us to be different.

What you say about yourself is important. A lot of Christians treat the Word of God like a book that they can pick and choose what they want to do. Sometimes we tend to let go of things we've heard for a long time. Sometimes, without thinking about it, we stop putting principles into practice that we used to firmly believe.

You might say, "Yeah, I've heard that. I know I should watch the words that come out of my mouth. I remember that but I'm deeper than that now." Let me just tell you that it doesn't get any deeper than watching what comes out of your mouth.

Matthew 16:13 says, "*When Jesus came into the coasts of Caesarea Philippi, he asked his disciples, saying, Whom do men say that I the Son of Man am?*" Notice that Jesus asked His disciples a very specific question. He asked them what outsiders, or non-believers, were saying about Him.

The disciples answered him. *"And they said, Some say that thou art John the Baptist: some, Elias; and others, Jeremias, or one of the prophets. But whom say ye that I am?"* (John 16:14-15).

Jesus asked another question. This time He asked them who *they* thought He was. Why would Jesus ask them that? Because He expected His own to have a different opinion about the issues of life than the rest of the world has. He expects the same of us today.

Think of it this way. If Jesus were to ask you what people are saying about the world's condition, you'd tell Him what they think based on what you've heard them say. Right?

Then He would ask you, "But what do *you* say?" When He asks you that, He expects you to have a different opinion, a different attitude, a different outlook, a different perspective, and different words coming out of your mouth than the rest of the world. Jesus doesn't want you to have the same opinions as the world. Your perspective should be much different from the people in the world who have no hope. If your outlook is the same, then you need to take inventory of your life and find out what's wrong. Ask yourself what's going on in your life that's causing you to limit God. All the world knows is limits and boundaries. That's what makes them ordinary. That's not true for you. You're not ordinary. You're set apart. You're extraordinary.

Breaking the Boundaries

You can't talk like the world and break the boundaries in your life. So many in the Body of Christ go to church every week faithfully, but by the time they get to the parking lot, they're talking the same way the world does. When you do that, you are allowing limitations to come into your life. How? By speaking things that are contrary to the Word of

God. You just simply cannot say what the world says and then expect to have what God's Word says.

Seeds of Limitation

The truth is that most of the limitations in your life are self-induced. They didn't come from God. God isn't keeping prosperity from you. He's not keeping success away from you. He's trying to get them *to you*. You just have to believe what He says instead of what the world says.

Most of the boundaries in your life are products of your environment, your culture, the way you were raised, or the people you associate with. They will produce limitations particularly if they don't line up with the Word of God.

Many of the boundaries in your life are products of your environment, your culture, the way you were raised, or the people you associate with.

What are seeds of limitation? Let me explain.

Ever since you were a small child, the way you thought was influenced by where you live, by your family and their beliefs, your friends, the media, and your culture. If you were brought up hearing things like, "God is trying to teach you something with this sickness," then it created a limitation in your life. If your parents said, "We could never afford that," then you probably grew up with a *lack mentality*. Those where seeds of limitation.

If your friends were always talking about their problems and being negative, then most likely you acted and thought like they did. For example, if your friends constantly say things like, "This is my life. It's just how it is. I can never get ahead." How do you think you'll respond the next time something negative happens in your life? You'll probably react the same way. You'll have placed another limitation on yourself.

Limitations, boundaries, or restrictions in your life did not come from God. God isn't the one who told you, "You can't have that, or you can't do that, or you can't be that." He'll never say that to you.

Doubt Limits God

We've seen that it's the devil who puts boundaries in your life, and it's you who accepts them in your life. Did you know that it's possible for you to limit God in your life? The answer is yes. He's an unlimited God, but His own people can limit Him from doing all that He wants to do in their lives.

Too many times instead of believing and trusting God, we doubt that He can or will really help us. When we doubt God and His willingness to help us, we limit Him and we tie His hands from intervening in our lives.

In the book of Exodus, there are many examples of God trying to help His people. He wanted them to bless them, but they had a hard time trusting Him. He was limited in His ability to intervene on their behalf many times simply because of their unbelief.

In Psalm 78:41 it says, "Yea, they turned back and tempted God, and limited the Holy One of Israel." God's people limited the Holy One of Israel. How many times do you suppose you've limited God?

If you study Psalm 78, you'll find out that the two primary ways the children of Israel limited God was by their negative talking and by their small thinking. They actually limited Him in their lives by how they thought and how they talked.

God's people limited the Holy One of Israel. How many times do you suppose you've limited God?

The primary way Christians limit God today is the same—by negative talking and small thinking. Where do you get all of this small thinking? Where do you get all of this negative talking? It comes from your environment, family, friends, and your culture. They have shaped the way you think and talk. How do you change the things in your life that have shaped you since birth? The Word of God is the only thing that makes this change in you.

Increase by Association

If you discover that you're somebody who limits God by your small thinking, then find people who think bigger than you and place yourself around them or under their influence. Spend time listening to them to see how they act, respond, and deal with situations that come up in their lives. This is the spiritual law called increase by association. You'll become like the people you hang around so choose people who are higher than you are in the things of God so you can come up to their level.

No matter how often God performed miracles in the Israelites' lives, the next time an issue came up they asked, "But can He do this?" No matter how many wonders He performed, no matter what He did on their behalf, when the next seemingly impossible situation came up they said, "Yes, but can He do this?"

The children of Israel never got past, "I wonder if He can." All God wanted was for them to trust Him as their One true source, but they couldn't get past wondering if He was capable. Is that you today? Are you constantly wondering if

God can deliver you? If so, He wants you to trust Him. At some point in your life you need to get to the place where it's not, "Can He?" but "He can and He will!"

Words Limit God

Negative talking and small thinking will build boundaries around you. When you complain about your circumstances, you're talking negative. When you talk negative, you're limiting God. When you limit God, you're obviously limiting yourself. See how all of this is related? When you choose to think things through in your own might and with your own ability instead of going to the Word, then you limit God, and He can't perform in your life the way He would like.

It's easy to get frustrated with God when things are not happening as quickly as you think they should. But the reality is that you could be the one who is stopping the blessing on your life because you have limited God with your negative talking and small thinking.

Verse 12 of Psalm 78 says, "Marvelous things did he in the sight of their fathers." Then it talks about all of the great things that God did like splitting the Red Sea. Don't you think if you'd witnessed that event, you'd have never been able to doubt God again? Can you imagine what it was like crossing through the Red Sea on dry ground? Think about it. One moment you're standing there looking at that sea and thinking you are in an impossible situation. What are you going to do? Pharaoh is coming up behind you, and he's either going to take you back into captivity or kill you where you stand. Talk about being between a rock and hard place. You're there. Now remember, you don't know God can split the Red Sea.

You haven't *read* Exodus, you're *living* Exodus.

The children of Israel didn't know that God could split the Red Sea. They'd never heard He could. So here they are. Standing there looking at the Red Sea and seeing a cloud of dust approaching from behind. Pharaoh is coming for them. What would you do? I mean, what's next? You know they had to be thinking that their end was near. Then suddenly, God split the Red sea. The Bible actually says that God split the Red Sea through the breath of His nostrils (Exodus 15:8).

On Dry Ground

The Red Sea split and they started walking across on dry ground. Just imagine that. The whole time they're seeing a wall of water on each side. Can you imagine walking through the sea with walls of water on both sides of you? Then, when you get on the other side, you see Pharaoh and his team charging after you. But God caused the wheels to fall off their chariots. The Bible says, "And they drove heavily," (Exodus 14:25). That's like trying to drive your car with no wheels on it. The next thing they see is the walls of the Red Sea coming back together. Now, if you'd been one of those Israelites on the other side watching all of this, do you think that you'd ever doubt God's ability again?

It may be hard to believe but we do the same thing to God all the time. How many times have you lost it when a crisis hit? It's easy to forget the things He did for you in the past when your present is in a mess. What do we automatically do? We start talking about what we see instead of what the Word says, and then we limit God. When you start thinking and making plans as if nothing is going to change, you're limiting God. If God has come through for you once, He can and will do it again! He wants to come through for you every time.

When you start thinking and making plans as if nothing is going to change, you're limiting God.

Not Hard for God

It seems no matter what God does for some people, they still don't know if He can do something about their next problem. They know He healed their headache, but they question whether or not He can heal the flu. Is it any harder for God to heal the flu than it is for Him to heal a headache? No. That's absurd. He's God. Nothing is too hard for God. They know He provided $25.00 for some groceries, but they question whether He can provide $200.00 for the electric bill. Is $200.00 any harder for God to come up with than $25.00? No. Money isn't an issue with God. He has more than enough to take care of all your financial needs.

My point is that no matter how many miracles God performs in some people's lives, they still talk negative and think small. Am I talking to you? God may have healed your body a year ago, but now all you know is that you're in pain. You know God doesn't want your life like that, but instead of speaking the Word, you're talking your sickness, and the truth is that God can't move in that atmosphere. That's exactly what happened to the children of Israel.

They knew God provided water for them,
but now they questioned whether or not
He could provide meat as well.

Psalm 78: 19-20 reads, *"Yea, they spake against God; they said, Can God furnish the table in the wilderness? Behold, he smote the rock, that the waters gushed out, and the streams overflowed; can he give bread also? Can he provide flesh for his people?"* They knew God provided water for them, but now they questioned whether or not He could provide meat

as well. The children of Israel were constantly question-
ing God's willingness and ability to move in their lives.
No matter how many marvelous things God did for them,
when the next impossible looking situation that came up in
their lives they doubted Him.

Sometimes you don't need the devil to cause problems
for you. All you need is a big mouth.

Murmuring

Sometimes you don't need the devil to cause problems for
you. All you need is a big mouth. A negative mouth will
get you in as much trouble as the devil can get you in. Let
me encourage you to check up on what's coming out of
your mouth. What are you confessing? Are you listening to
the media all the time and reading negative things? Then
you need to at least give the Word of God equal time. Jesus
said out of the abundance of the heart the mouth speaks
(Luke 6:45). Pay close attention to what you put into your
heart. Why? What's in your heart will come out of your
mouth.

Some people say, "God's God. He can just do anything He wants to do." Well, if that's true, then why isn't everybody on the planet already experiencing salvation? God is not going to make anybody get saved. God gave everyone a will. We all have the right to choose. You can choose to go to hell, and God will protect your right to go—even though you're a fool if you do when that's not what God wants for you.

Notice the Bible says that if you confess with your mouth and believe in your heart that God has raised Jesus from the dead thou shall be saved (Romans 10:9-10). The implication is that it's your responsibility.

> *God gives you the choice and then gives you an inside tip—choose life because it's better than death. Choose the blessing because it's better than the curse.*

Why doesn't God make you forgive? Why doesn't He make people go to church? He's capable of doing it, wouldn't you say? He is God after all. But, He's not going to MAKE anybody do anything. He gave us the choice.

He said, "I've set before you life and death, blessing and cursing." Then He says, "Choose life," (Deuteronomy 30:19). God gives you the choice and then gives you an inside tip—choose life because it's better than death. Choose the blessing because it's better than the curse. But, He is not going to make you do anything. It's your choice.

If God was going to make people do things, then why didn't He make the Israelites obey? They **murmured and complained** about everything all the time. He didn't make them straighten up. He gave them the choice. He let them walk in disobedience, and they paid the price for it. They knew the consequences if they didn't obey God's laws, but He didn't force them to obey. He gave them the choice.

He Can and He Will

There has to come a time in your life when you stop murmuring and complaining, and rejoice because you know God will rescue you. You should reach a point when you no longer ask, "Can He?" but you shout at the top of your voice, "He can!" The Israelites didn't get that. They spoke negative words and thought small. By limiting Him, He was not able to do all that He wanted to do for them. No matter how many marvelous things He did for them, it wasn't enough to cause them to trust Him. Their small thinking robbed them of the many more miracles that He wanted to do in their lives.

Final Authority

Too many of God's people today are limiting Him simply because they're allowing what everybody else says to be final authority. If you're ever going to have God's best in your life, you have to decide that God's Word and nothing else will be final authority in your life. The negative report that the doctor gave you is not the final authority. It may be fact, but the Word is a higher form of truth. It is above the report of the doctor. The sickness in your body has to bow to the Word every time you apply it to your life.

A good example of the Word being final authority is found in the story of the Roman Centurion who came to Jesus about his servant who was grievously tormented. In Matthew 8:5-8, it says:

"And when Jesus was entered into Capernaum, there came unto him a centurion, beseeching him, And saying, Lord, my servant lieth at home sick of the palsy, grievously tormented. And Jesus saith unto him, I will come and heal him. The centurion answered and said, Lord, I am not worthy that thou shouldest come under my roof: but speak the word only, and my servant shall be healed."

All this man needed was for Jesus to speak the Word. As far as the Roman Centurion was concerned, Jesus' word was his final authority. He didn't need to see something or feel something first. No, the Word was all that was necessary. He didn't need Jesus to come to his house and lay hands on his servant. In his mind, all he needed was for Jesus to speak the Word. He knew that the Word would heal his servant.

Jesus was so impressed with the Roman Centurion that He turned to His disciples and said, "Verily I say unto you, I have not found so great faith, no, not in Israel," (verse 10). How would you like for Jesus to be impressed with your faith like that? He will be as soon as you make God's Word final authority in your life.

V.

REFUSE TO SETTLE FOR WHAT THE WORLD SAYS

I know times are tough for a lot of people. I don't pretend that there aren't problems. People are unemployed at unprecedented rates and are losing everything they worked for. Baby Boomers like me were told that if we worked hard and saved, by the time we retired we'd have a nice nest egg. But a lot of good people who've saved their whole lives have lost those nest eggs. I'm not suggesting that you pretend that nothing like that is happening in the world. I'm not telling you to pretend that life is really great when it isn't.

When your house is about to be foreclosed faith doesn't say, "My mortgage isn't past due. I don't even believe in mortgages." That's not faith. Faith looks at the negative situation then finds the solution in the Word and refuses to let go of it until it's fulfilled.

The life of faith isn't a life of pretense. It's a life where you see the problems, and then you use the Word of God to attack them. That's why the Bible says, "And from the days of John the Baptist until now the kingdom of heaven suffereth violence, and the violent take it by force," (Matthew

11:12). You have to get violent and wield the Word of God with force.

You have to do everything in your power to keep the world out and the Word in if you're going to win.

I don't care what's happening in the economy, we don't have to be restricted with the world's restrictions. We don't have to be confined by their confinements. If everyone in the country was getting a pay cut, it wouldn't have to happen to you or me.

Don't pay so much attention to what the world is saying, because the world will try and build boundaries around you. You may be hearing too much negative news and not enough of the Word. If so, turn off your television. Stop hanging around people who talk gloom and doom. You have to do everything in your power to keep the *world out* and the *Word in* if you're going to win.

Never Settle

No matter what's happening with the economy, no matter what's happening with your company or your family, *refuse to settle for what the world says!* One of the primary reasons most Christians fail to live an extraordinary life is that they're willing to settle for less. At least, until they hear the truth. That's what happened to me. The moment I heard the truth about what God purchased for me, I wasn't willing to settle for anything less. Once I knew that God promised something, it didn't matter how many people bellowed about it. If God said I could have something, I wasn't willing to live without it. I knew it might not happen overnight, but that didn't bother me. I have lots of nights. I realized that it might not happen in a week, or a month or a year, but everybody had better get out of my way because I was going for it and I wasn't willing to quit. I refused to give up. That simply wasn't an option for me. I refused to be deterred from having everything God said I could have. In order to break through the barriers in my own life, I reached for God's promises.

As soon as I saw what the Word of God said about my situation, there was no holding me back. I set my face like flint on the promises. If the Word said I could have it—

that settled it. However, there were other steps I had to take in order not to settle for less than God's best.

Forget the Past

I had to forget the past. In Philippians 3: 13-14 Paul said, "Brethren, I count not myself to have apprehended: but this one thing I do, forgetting those things which are behind, and reaching forth unto those things which are before, I press toward the mark for the prize of the high calling of God in Christ Jesus."

I'm letting it go and reaching for what lies ahead.

In my pressing, I had to forget the past. I forgot the way I lived before. I forgot how all of my relatives had lived. I forgot how my immediate family lived. I said, "I'm forgetting all that. I'm letting it go and reaching for what lies ahead." I let go of the past. I refused to allow how I'd thought and how I'd lived in the past affect my present or my future. My heart shouted, *Why settle for the ordinary when God promised extraordinary?*

I refused to continue living a mediocre life. The word *mediocre* means commonplace, adequate, run of the mill, inferior, tolerable, passable. That's what most people are willing to settle for—*mediocre*. Is that how you want to live?

Most Christians today want to do the bare minimum. If you're a student studying for a test, do you study just to pass or do you study to earn an A? If your goal is just to pass, you're mediocre. Striving for the best grade you can possibly get is reaching for the extraordinary.

"Well, Brother Jerry, no one in my family has ever done well in school."

That might be true, but it doesn't have to be true for you. Look at it as a boundary that God has given you the power to break through. The Holy Spirit is your teacher and He knows how to help you learn and make good grades. Forget the past. Forget every bad grade you've made. Forget the bad report cards your daddy got. Forget the sad stories from all of your relatives. Break the boundaries in your life!

Too often, people have a mediocre mentality and they're happy to just get by. In other words, they're satisfied with mediocre. If you're living a mediocre life today, it's because you have a mediocre mindset. If you're not willing to press for the extraordinary, it's because you're willing to settle for a run of the mill, average, commonplace, tolerable and passable kind of life.

No one said that living an extraordinary life would be easy. In order to do so, you have to refuse to settle for what the world says and become determined to have what God says instead.

Accept Correction

Sometimes God will correct you and put you back on the right path. If somebody shows you why you're living beneath your status in God, are you going to get mad at them? A lot of people do. They take offense and get mad at the very person God sent to help them. The Bible says to reprove, rebuke and encourage (2 Timothy 4:2).

Did you notice that two out of the three of those weren't pleasant? It's no fun to be reproved and rebuked. However, God requires it because He knows human nature. He understands that we need rebuking from time to time. Everybody has been corrected at one time or another. If you take that correction and do it, you'll grow. If you get mad or hurt, the Bible calls you a fool (Proverbs 10:8). You're limiting yourself from receiving the life that God wants you to have.

Keep in mind that the only reason God would rebuke you is to elevate you. He wants you to go higher. He wants you to break free from the limitations that have held you back. Stop being willing to settle for far less than what God wants you to have.

One reason some people never get over their past is because they can't forgive themselves. They want to keep bringing up the mistakes they made. My friend, that's settling for less. I don't know about you, but I'm not willing to settle for less, not when I know what Jesus went through to offer me the extraordinary. He took stripes on His back for me. He hung on the cross for me. He died for me. He paid the penalty in Satan's domain for three days and nights and then He came up out of the grave, raised victoriously, for me.

If Jesus was standing in front of you right now, He'd say to you, "I don't care what you do or how much you mess up, just repent, get back on track and start living for Me. Put Me first place in your life and I'll bring you out of the ordinary and into the extraordinary!" Isn't that great news? You're always a candidate for the extraordinary life.

Let me ask you something. Why do you deserve an extraordinary life? It's because God is full of mercy and loving kindness. God is a gracious God. The moment you repent, as far as God is concerned, your sin is in the sea of forgetfulness. He doesn't remember it. If you said to Him, "God I'm sorry again for what I did," He'd have to say, "What are you talking about? Now go get back what belongs to you. And don't settle for anything less, because you're *mine!*"

Who hasn't messed up? Who hasn't sinned? Who hasn't compromised a time or two? Who cares what level it was? Sin is sin. Compromise is compromise. The main thing is that you have a Father that you can go to and say, "I've sinned, forgive me, I repent, I make an about face." When you do that, God will say, "You're forgiven; now leave that ordinary life and step up to the extraordinary."

Let's face it, if you believe the Word and trust that God's blessings are on you, why would you ever fall into a pity party?

You'll never live an extraordinary life unless you give up feeling sorry for yourself. No more pity parties. Let's face it, if you believe the Word and trust that God's blessings are on you, why would you ever fall into a pity party? You've got to see them for what they are—a huge boundary that separates you from God's extraordinary best. When you start feeling sorry for yourself, you need to pay attention. You just stepped into a demonic trap.

Lack of Knowledge

The Bible says in Hosea 4:6, "My people perish for a lack of knowledge." I like to say that you live beneath your privileges for a lack of knowledge. When I read in John 10:10 where it says that Jesus has come that we might have life and life abundantly, I asked myself, *Why I would settle for anything less than abundant living? Why would I settle for ordinary when I can have extraordinary?* Why are you settling for ordinary when God wants you to experience His extraordinary? Most likely it's because of a lack of knowledge.

Throughout the Bible the scriptures prove that God wants His children to not only have their needs met, but to have more than enough. Why? So that when your needs are met, you'll have enough left over to meet someone else's.

"If you're going to go around confessing the blessings of Abraham are yours, then you have to accept the call of Abraham."

Abraham was a good example of this. God took him from his father's land, and blessed him until he became very wealthy. Abraham always had enough left over to be a blessing to someone else.

The Lord said to me many years ago, "If you're going to go around confessing the blessings of Abraham are yours, then you have to accept the call of Abraham." The call of Abraham was this: I'll bless you and make you a blessing. The call of Abraham was to bless all the families of the earth. God said, "Through you all families of the earth will be blessed."

Far Over and Above

That's exactly what Paul was talking about in Ephesians 3:20, "Now to Him Who, by (in consequence of) the [action of His] power that is at work within us, is able to [carry out His purpose and] do superabundantly, far over and above all that we [dare] ask or think [infinitely beyond our highest prayers, desires, thoughts, hopes, or dreams]" (Amplified).

Are you beginning to see that God wants to do extraordinary things in your life?

In the Message Bible that verse says, "God can do anything, you know—far more than you could ever imagine or guess or request in your wildest dreams!"

I love that. I can dream big. How about you?

He said that God can do superabundantly, far above all that you could possibly dream or ask or request. Then it says, "According to the power that worketh within you." What power is he talking about? The power he's talking about is the power to *comprehend* it. The ability to conceive the idea and the truth that God wants you to live an extraordinary life. If you can't conceive it, then you can't receive it.

If you can grasp it, if you can comprehend it, if you can conceive it, then God said you can have it.

To *comprehend* means to grasp and to lay hold upon. You may have to stretch your faith to be able to see yourself living an extraordinary life, but if you can grasp it, if you can comprehend it, if you can conceive it, then God said you can have it.

One meaning in the dictionary for the word *conceive* is to become pregnant. I can say "I've become pregnant with the vision of extraordinary instead of ordinary." Do you realize the word *know,* in its strongest form, literally means intercourse? When you're pursuing God and you're pursuing the knowledge of God, then a spiritual intercourse takes place—the mingling of two lives. When that happens, you'll walk away pregnant with God's ideas, God's dreams and His desires for your life.

Four Minute Mile

Many things have happened in sports that the world said was impossible. It amazes me how somebody always sets out to prove the experts wrong. That's what happened with the four-minute mile. All the experts said it couldn't be done, but a man from England decided that he was going to break it. He studied human anatomy and nutrition and prepared himself to break that barrier, just to prove that it could be broken. He tried and failed. He tried and failed. He tried and failed, but he wouldn't give up.

One day he broke through that boundary. As soon as he did it, other people were breaking it right and left. Today the four-minute mile barrier doesn't exist, all because one man refused to let the experts limit him. If you want to live an extraordinary life, you've got to stop listening to others, even the experts, and give your full attention to God's Word.

The Word of God is what makes you different from everybody else. Without it, you're ordinary and subject to the world. But with it, you're unlimited and extraordinary. God wants your very life to become an evangelistic tool so that people can just watch the way you live and become attracted to the God you serve.

It's a lot better to represent God in times like this by excelling rather than going under. Do you want to reach wealthy and successful people for God? Then you have to stop defining yourself by the world's standards. Wealthy people are attracted by wealthy people. Successful people hang around successful people. They don't like boundaries. They push through boundaries. Challenges get them fired up. They don't quit when they see an obstacle. Instead, like the man who beat the four-minute mile barrier, they figure out how to leap over it.

Find Favor

If you've made a firm decision that you're not going to settle for mediocre, one of the best ways to obliterate the boundaries in your life is to get a deeper understanding of the favor of God. Other than becoming a new creation and being made the righteousness of God, this is one of the greatest revelations I've received from the Word. God wants to pour out His favor on your life, and when the favor of God is on your life, you have no boundaries.

Favor means kind regard, friendly disposition, support, defense, vindication, promotion, justification, benevolence, acts of grace and goodwill, advantage, partiality, preferential treatment and convenience afforded for success. That's the favor of God.

"Favor is when people say, 'No!',
and circumstances say, 'No!',
but I say, 'Yes!'"

The Lord once said to me, "There are things going on in your world today that only the favor of God will get you over." So I asked, "What's Your definition of favor?"

I was shocked at what He said, and yet it made sense. He said, "Favor is when people say, 'No!', and circumstances say, 'No!', but I say, 'Yes!'" That's favor."

When everything around you is screaming, "No!" but God says, "Yes!" that's favor. The Bible says that God's favor is on your life. However, you're the only one who can determine the level to which you walk in it.

Psalm 5:11-12 says, "But let all those that put their trust in thee rejoice: let them ever shout for joy, because thou defendest them: let them also that love thy name be joyful in thee. For thou, LORD, wilt bless the righteous; with favour wilt thou compass him as with a shield."

The Amplified Bible says it this way, "You will surround him with goodwill (pleasure and favor)."

Surrounded by Favor

You are surrounded by the favor of God and that's why you can't fail. That might sound bold to someone who doesn't know their covenant, but it's not egotistical. I'm just quoting the Bible. The Bible says He will surround you with His favor. If you're surrounded by the favor of God and if you know how to walk in it, then you can't fail.

Job 10:12 says, "Thou hast granted me life and favour." God has bestowed His favor upon you.

Psalm 30:5 in the Amplified Bible says, "His favor is for a lifetime." The favor of God is there for your entire lifetime. He wants you to walk in His favor every day. He's given it to you and expects you to take hold of it and walk in it.

If you've made Jesus the Lord of your life,
that same favor is on you.

Speaking of the children of Israel, Psalm 44:3 says, "For they got not the land in possession by their own sword, neither did their own arm save them: but thy right hand, and thine arm, and the light of thy countenance, because thou hadst a favour unto them." The Amplified Bible says that the reason they won this battle and got the land without having to lift a finger for it was because, "You were favorable toward and did delight in them."

A Chosen People

God chose the Israelites out of all of the people on this earth and said, "I'm going to show My favor on them." If you've made Jesus the Lord of your life, that same favor is on you. He has chosen to lift you up high and bestow support, defense, promotion and preferential treatment on you. The next time something good happens to you, don't think it happened by chance. Always acknowledge God's favor on your life. The more you do, the more you'll see it manifest.

The Lord once said to me, "When you know the favor of God is on you, then it'll win the battle for you."

In Psalm 106:4, the Psalmist cried out, "Remember me, O LORD, with the favour that thou bearest unto thy people." The word *bear* here means support, sustain, keep afloat, deliver and bring forth.

The Psalmist was saying, "God I want that favor on my life that comes from You, and if I have Your favor, it will keep me afloat. It will sustain me. It will deliver me and bring me out of any situation."

Proverbs 14:9, 11 says, "Among the upright there is the favor of God. The house of the wicked shall be overthrown, but the tent of the upright shall flourish." When the favor of God is on your life, you flourish. Because of God's favor, you will walk with an uplifted face (Psalm 89:17). That means you can walk with your head held high in what the world calls bad times because you have the favor of God. That is extraordinary.

The favor of God will do things for you that nothing else can do. It will open doors that no man can shut. It will give you promotions when you don't have seniority. It will give you jobs when you don't even have the expertise. The favor of God will keep your job when everybody else is getting laid off. The favor of God will put you in a house when nobody else is getting a house. The favor of God will sell your house when houses can't be sold. Not only that, it will get you a great price! Favor can do what nothing else can do. It's one of the major tools that God has given you to break through boundaries.

It Will Put You Over

Favor means that you don't go under, you go over. Get a revelation of the fact that you're not ordinary. God created for you to be extraordinary. Remind yourself everyday that you walk in God's favor. You have something on your life that the rest of the world doesn't have. However, you have to make a demand on the favor of God. I'm not talking about demanding something from God; I'm talking about you placing a demand on the favor that God has placed on your life. Start confessing that the favor of God is present in your life everyday and expect it to manifest.

What makes us different from the rest of the world? Why don't we have the world's limitations? It's because of the Word, the blessing and the favor of the Lord on our lives. The blessing of God can do what money can't do. The favor of God can do what fame can't do. When you have the blessing of God and the favor of God, you don't need anything else because they will produce everything you need. God has given you everything you need to live an extraordinary life, so refuse to settle for anything less.

VI.

DETERMINE YOUR DESTINY

What does the local and national news have to say about the economy right now? You don't have to watch it very often to know that nothing good is being reported. If that's all you listen to, then you've placed another limitation on your life. You're limited to what the world tells you. They'll tell you that you can't prosper in this economy. They'll tell you that times are rough, and they're just going to get rougher. They'll say that the jobless rate is high, and is probably going get higher. Those, my friend, are limits.

Does your future look ordinary or extraordinary? Do you see yourself as a winner or a loser? I want you to know that no matter what your future looks like right now, this chapter has the potential to change your life forever. If you'll apply the financial principles that I'm about to share with you, it'll take you from being ordinary in the financial realm to experiencing the extraordinary.

Are you tired of your finances being limited? I know I was. The time came when I wasn't only tired of my financial situation; I knew something had to change. I needed God to show up in my finances. I was in debt. I was broke. My financial situation wasn't good. I know what it's like to struggle financially. I understand what those pressures feel like, but I can also tell you how to change it. Those are just distant memories to me now because God taught me about His plan for my finances. He taught me the principles that I needed to know to take me from being ordinary and very limited where my money was concerned to living in the overflow and abundance of His blessings. God showed up in my finances. And, He wants to do the same for you.

"So how do I change it, Brother Jerry?"

This is how you change it—the law of seedtime and harvest. Anyone who practices this law will prosper every time. It's not only His promise; it's a spiritual law.

Anyone who practices this law will prosper every time. It's not only His promise; it's a spiritual law.

The Whole Earth Revolves Around This Law

The first thing you need to know about the law of seed time and harvest is this: everything on this planet revolves around that law. It has everything to do with how your life turns out. I like to say it this way: *The seeds you sow determine how far you'll go in God's plan for your life.*

Genesis 1:29 says, "And God said, 'Behold, I have given you every herb bearing seed, which is upon the face of all the earth, and every tree, in the which is the fruit of a tree yielding seed; to you it shall be for meat.'" The word *meat* means provision. God says "I have given you every herb bearing seed, and for you it shall be for provision."

God once asked me, "After creating man, what were the first two gifts I gave him?"

I didn't know.

I knew God was going somewhere with this so I needed to figure it out. I went to Genesis, chapter 1, and said, "Gift number one was dominion and authority. Number two is every herb bearing seed."

I learned that God gave man these things: dominion, authority, and seed. We'll talk about dominion and authority later, but in this chapter I want to focus on seed.

It's Who You Are and What You Do

From the very beginning of time, God intended for you to be a sower of seed. Sowing seed is not some side issue. *Sowing seed is actually how God intended for you to have your life sustained.* God wants you to be a sower. A sower should be who you are and what you do.

I'm a preacher. It's what I am, and it's what I do. Before this, I was trained in the automotive business and my profession was auto repair. Although that was my profession, in the mind of God I've been a preacher since the foundation of the earth, because that's what He created me to be. When I discovered God's plan for my life, I gave up the other profession.

From the very beginning, God intended for everyone reading this book to be a sower. Sowing represents what you are and what you do. It's the way God intended for your life to be sustained. You may be a lawyer, a doctor, or a mechanic, but to God that's a side issue. To Him that's not how you sustain your life. *Your job is not supposed to be what you do to earn a living. God considers your job as what you do to earn a giving. Your job is nothing more than a means for you to have seed to sow.*

Your personal income can be far greater than what your job pays you. Why? It's because you don't have to limit yourself to a paycheck if you are a sower. Your income is determined by your sowing, not by what somebody pays you. You may say, "I'm on a fixed income. I don't have the avenues for other income the way you do." Well, if that's your confession, it's limiting you. You don't have to live on a fixed income. How do you know you don't have other avenues? From the very beginning, God intended for you and me to have our lives sustained by the seeds we sow.

God has called you to be a sower.

Having a large library of law books doesn't make you a lawyer. Having a barn doesn't make you a farmer no more than you giving an offering only on Sunday makes you a sower. When God calls a person a sower, He intends for them to sow 24 hours a day, seven days a week. A sower understands that their thoughts, their words, their attitudes, their actions, and everything they possess are seeds.

God has called you to be a sower.

They're constantly aware that their thoughts are seeds, their words are seeds, and their actions are seeds. Those seeds impact their life either for good or bad. A sower is someone who understands the power of seeds and plants them every day of their life. If you want to live an extraordinary life without boundaries, you must recognize and understand the power of seeds.

You Always Have Seed

God said, "I've given you seed." **You may not always have what you need, but you are never without seed.** Why? Because God said, "I've given you seed."

Can God lie? No. In that case, somewhere you have seed to sow. You may not always have what you need at the moment, but you are never without the seed that will produce it. Your seed will always produce what you need.

You may not have money to give. That's okay. Seed can be prayer. When I first learned these things, I wanted to give, but I didn't have any money so I started sowing prayer time. I sowed an hour a day in prayer, and, before long, the money came so that I could sow a financial seed. You're never without seed, but sometimes you have to look for it.

According to Genesis, from the very beginning of time God intended for His children to be sowers. It's how our lives are supposed to be sustained. God wants you to know that through sowing you alone determine your own destiny. Through the law of seed time and harvest you take charge of your life. You take charge of your financial future. God has given you the privilege and the right to take charge of your destiny.

My thoughts, words, attitude, and actions were the reason my life was in a downhill spiral. It was a result of the seeds I was sowing.

Before I came to the Lord I had no idea that the way my life had turned out was a result of the seeds I had sown.

Like most people, I just woke up every morning wondering what would happen next. I had no idea that I had the ability to take charge of my own destiny. I didn't know that my thoughts, my words, my attitude, and my actions had everything to do with the way my life had become. My thoughts, words, attitude, and actions were the reason my life was in a downhill spiral. It was a result of the seeds I was sowing.

Have you ever heard the phrase, "The reason they're living that way is because of all of those wild oats they sowed?" How about, "They live that way because they're reaping what they sowed." Isn't it amazing how so many people believe that if they sow negative seeds, it'll produce a negative harvest, but if you try to convince them they can turn that around and sow positive seeds they don't believe it.

*Learn how you can take charge of your destiny
through the seeds that you sowed.*

I was sowing negative seeds back then and didn't even know it. I didn't have a clue. I was just doing what I'd been taught to do. I was doing what I saw others do. I was talking the problems just like I heard everybody else do. I was living the way my Dad lived, and he was in the same mess. However, when I began to understand seedtime and harvest, my life radically changed.

In Mark 4, we see the parable of the sower. It says that the sower sows the Word. I heard the Word, and it was such a revelation to me that I couldn't get enough of it. I was a man on a quest. Many times when my family went to bed, I'd be up all night studying the Bible and endeavoring to learn how I could take charge of my destiny through the seeds that I sowed.

Seeds Aren't Only Money

People often think that when you're talking about seeds you're automatically talking about money. But seed time and harvest is not limited to money. You can sow your time to someone. You can sow help for someone. You can sow prayer. You can sow kind words or helpful deeds. Those are all different ways to sow.

If you change the way that you think,
then you will change the way you live.

One of the first things I learned was that my thoughts were seeds. Once I learned that, what did I do? I began changing the way I thought. Everything in our lives begins as a thought. Buying this book began as a thought. Your house began as a thought. Your car began as a thought. That makes them a seed. Everything begins with a seed. It's the law of Genesis. Thoughts are seeds. ***If you change the way that you think, then you will change the way you live.***

Proverbs 23:7 says, "For as a man thinketh in his heart, so is he." That simply means that your life will go in the direction of your most dominate thoughts. What do you think about? Do you think about failure? Do you think about how you never seem to have enough? People get off into sin or crime because they meditate on the wrong thoughts. You might not think that watching a TV show can affect you, but after a while, it will. After a while, you'll become desensitized to the sin you're watching and it won't seem so bad.

The person who gets into a life of crime doesn't start off with those intentions. They begin by thinking; I could steal that and get away with it. They might shrug off the thought at first, but it'll come back. They'll meditate on it a little more. The next thing you know they have a mental picture of themselves doing it. In time they find themselves sitting in a prison cell; their life has become the result of what began as a thought. A thought can grow into a living thing—an action—and that makes your thoughts seeds. Anything that has the potential of growing is a seed.

You think if you just sow money, you're going to become wealthy. But if you haven't done anything with your thoughts, actions, and attitude, your money isn't going to grow.

Maybe the reason that you're not experiencing the kind of results that you should in your finances is because you're only getting one part of this. You think if you just sow money, you're going to become wealthy. But if you haven't done anything with your thoughts, actions, and attitude, your money isn't going to grow. Your thoughts, your words, your attitudes, and your actions could be negating the money you sowed. If you don't get them in line, then your money seed will have weeds growing which will choke it out.

I started by filling my mind and heart with the Word of God until God's thoughts became my thoughts. The Bible is God's thoughts in print. So begin filling your mind and your heart with the Word of God until His thoughts become your thoughts.

Words Are Seeds

The second thing I learned about seeds was that my words were seeds. Jesus said in Matthew 12:35, "A good man out of the good treasure of the heart bringeth forth good things: and an evil man out of the evil treasure bringeth forth evil things." That simply means positive words produce positive results, and negative words produce negative results. If you want your life to go the way God has planned for you, you're going to have to watch what you say. You can't go around talking doubt and unbelief all week and then on Sunday say what the Word says. It won't work. It won't produce the results that you want. You'll continue to live an ordinary life full of limitations like everyone else.

You're exactly what you have been talking.

Proverbs 6:2 says, "Thou art snared with the words of thy mouth, thou art taken with the words of thy mouth." Your words are vehicles, they are carriers, and by taking charge of your mouth, you can take charge of your destiny. If you don't like where you are in life, think about what you have been saying, because you're exactly what you have been talking.

Have you ever said, "We never seem to have enough to pay our bills? Or "I get sick this same time every year?" Well, you are experiencing exactly what you say. So quit saying it!

Your Attitude is Seed

The third thing you have to work on is your attitude. Your attitude is a reflection of what's really going on deep down inside of you. You can fake it for a while, but your attitude will give you up every time. It happens because your attitude reflects what you're really thinking.

If your attitude is negative, it's because you don't really expect anything good to happen to you. You don't really believe God's Word yet. You're not thoroughly convinced and persuaded that God meant what He said. If you're not convinced that God can be depended upon, your attitude will reveal it. If that's you, just spend more time in the Word and less time in the world. Quality time with God will revolutionize your attitude.

If you sow a good attitude, then you'll reap a good harvest. There are times when you can defeat the devil with nothing more than your attitude. Just decide that no matter what he does, no matter what he says, it's not going to affect your positive attitude.

Whether you realize it or not, your attitude dictates your actions.

Psalm 27:14 says, "My expectation is from Him." The more time you spend with God then obviously the more positive your attitude and expectations will be. Whether you realize it or not, your attitude dictates your actions. People with negative attitudes tend to act negatively. They can't help it. It's simply a spiritual law. A negative attitude along with negative actions always attracts negative people and negative results, and these will produce limits and boundaries in your life.

A negative attitude along with negative actions always attracts negative people and negative results, and these will produce limits and boundaries in your life.

Get the Chaos Out of Your Life

This planet revolves around the law of seed time and harvest. You can't get around it. In Genesis 1:2, it says the earth was void and full of darkness. In the literal Hebrew that means chaos. The world was in chaos. It was not the way God intended it to be when He created it.

The only way you can get the chaos out of your life is to learn the law of seed time and harvest. That's how important this law is. In order to take charge of your life you've got to take charge of your words, your thoughts, your attitude, and your actions. It's the only way.

Everything you own is a seed. The world calls them assets, but God calls them seeds.

What You Own Isn't Yours

Years ago I also discovered that everything I have in the way of material possessions are seeds. God has wrapped your life in seeds. Everything you own is a seed. The world calls them assets, but God calls them seeds. Some are bigger than others, but they are all seeds.

Several years ago, I asked the Lord, "Why is it important that I live debt free?"

"So that everything you have is a seed," He said. "If somebody else owns it, and you're still paying for it, then it's not a seed that you can sow."

God intended for you to be a sower of seed. That's the reason He wants you to be debt free. You can't sow something you don't own. Borrowing money isn't a sin, and neither is being in debt, but it's not God's best for your life, and it certainly limits you. God wants you to have more seed so you can be a greater blessing. Being in debt puts a boundary on you. Debt puts limits on your ability to sow.

Once again, God intended for you to be a sower. He wants you to get up every day of your life and ask, "Where am I going to sow today?" With that attitude what kind of harvest do you think you will you receive tomorrow?

Genesis 1:11 says that every seed produces after its own kind. That means apples produce apples. Oranges produce oranges. Money produces money. I don't understand why that's so hard for people to comprehend. I sow my money, so I have more money. You sow money, you reap money. This is God's way for you to be able to take charge of your financial destiny. The seeds you sow determine how far you go and that includes financially.

*If you're down to your last dollar,
don't you dare spend it! Sow it!*

Sow, Sow, Sow

If you're struggling financially right now, the worst thing you can do is withhold seed. If you're down to your last dollar, don't you dare spend it! Sow it! By sowing it, you're setting yourself up for a financial breakthrough.

The Seeding Seed

When I was a younger I spent time with my grandfather who was a farmer. At harvest time my grandfather always took the best corn and put it in the barn. He took the next best corn to the market, and we ate what was left over.

One day I said, "Grandpa, why do you always put the best corn in the barn?

"That's for next year's crop."

What was he saying? Put your best seed in the ground.

That's what Genesis 1:28 calls the seeding seed. The seeding seed is your best seed. You don't eat your best seed. Don't consume it—sow it. If you're struggling financially, the worst thing you can do is withhold your seed.

Let It Go

Proverbs 11:24 says, "There is that scattereth, and yet increaseth; and there is that withholdeth more than is meet, but it tendeth to poverty." If you withhold when you should be sowing, it will lead to poverty. Your circumstances will get worse. Why? It's because God intended for you to be a sower. It's the way that He intended for you to have your life sustained.

> *I know this doesn't make sense to your natural mind, but the key to increasing your finances is to scatter.*

The world doesn't understand this. They say, "If you haven't got much, then you better hold on to it because you never know what's going to happen." God says, "Give and it will be given unto you," (Luke 6:38). I know this doesn't make sense to your natural mind, but the key to increasing your finances is to scatter (Proverbs 11:24). And this isn't talking about just sowing once. You must keep on sowing for the rest of your life. Your life should be spent sowing. It's a continuous cycle.

I want to encourage you to get up every morning and look for an opportunity to sow something, not only for your own benefit but for the benefit of others. Whose fault is it that I'm blessed? Mine, because I obey the Word, and I sow. All I'm doing is what God intended for every man to do.

Have you ever noticed that seed time and harvest didn't begin after the fall of man? Seed time and harvest isn't a curse. It's how you get blessed. It came into existence when God created man. "Behold I give you the authority to take charge. Now, here's some seed." Therefore the way you take charge is to become a sower and do it for the rest of your life. That's the way God intended to provide for you.

Two Promises for Sowers

There are two things that God has promised to sowers in 2 Corinthians 9:10. "And [God] Who provides seed for the sower and bread for eating will also provide and multiply your [resources for] sowing." First, you'll never be without seed. God always provides seed for the sower. The worst day of your life, you'll still have a seed. It may only be the ability to walk up to somebody and say, "You're going to make it. I just wanted to encourage you today." But that's still seed. So if that's all you've got, sow it.

The second thing He promises a sower is that He will increase their resources for sowing. You'll never be without seed, and if you become someone who practices this all of your life, then He promises that He will continually increase your resources for sowing.

What you have sown will create such prosperity in your life that you'll be able to sow bigger and bigger and more and more. It's unending. It's unlimited. The most beautiful thing about this law is this: it knows no race, no background, no limits, and no boundaries. All it says is, "I was put here by God to work for you."

Genesis 8:22 says, "As long as the earth remaineth, seedtime and harvest shall not cease." As long as you're on this planet, you might as well face it, this law is at work. It's either working for you or against you. But it's working. Even when you say, "I don't believe that," it's working.

You Can't Out Give God

You can't out give God. Remember, God is not trying to keep things from you. He's trying to get things to you. It probably won't happen the way you think it will, but He is working for you. The law of seed time and harvest is always in action.

Your faith hasn't reached supreme expression until you've offered something significant.

In the book of James, it says, "Faith without works is dead." Faith without corresponding actions is dead or void of power. A good example of this is when Abraham offered up Isaac. The Bible says Abraham's faith reached supreme expression when he offered Isaac. How would you like for your faith to reach supreme expression? It is only when your faith reaches that level that it truly impresses God. Your faith hasn't reached supreme expression until you've offered something significant. God has tied faith and sowing together. "Was not our forefather Abraham [shown to be] justified (made acceptable to God) by [his] works when he brought to the altar as an offering his [own] son Isaac? You see that [his] faith was cooperating with his works, and [his] faith was completed and reached its supreme expression [when he implemented it] by [good] works" James 2:21-22 (Amplified Bible).

Our entire planet revolves around the law of seed time and harvest. The law of seed time and harvest is working all the time whether you realize it or not. It's the greatest tool you'll ever need to be a success in this life. Do you want to break the limits off of your life? Sow seed. Do you want to be a success? Sow seed. How can you live in the extraordinary? Become a sower. Ordinary people don't live like this.

If you don't like the path your life is on, then sow seeds to change your future!

With your God-given authority and the sowing of your seed, you determine your destiny. No one can keep you down when you practice the law of seed time and harvest. So keep doing what the Word says and refuse to be limited by what's going on around you. *You* determine your destiny.

VII.

TAKE CHARGE!

God didn't leave you on the earth hopeless and powerless. He gave you the same authority that Jesus has. He has given you all the tools you need to live an extraordinary, limitless life through Him. It's time for you to take charge of your life.

Genesis 1:28 says, "And God blessed them, and God said unto them, Be fruitful, and multiply, and replenish the earth, and subdue it: and have dominion over the fish of the sea, and over the fowl of the air, and over every living thing that moveth upon the earth." The Message translation says, "Take charge." God expects you to take charge of your life.

The First Gift

The first gift that God gave to man was dominion and authority. Just think about that for a minute. Mediate on it. God gave you authority over every thing on this earth. That means any circumstance or trial that comes your way, you have the power to overcome it. God gave you the authority and the ability to rule over every situation in your life.

In Genesis 1:26 it says, "And God said, Let us make man in our image, after our likeness." The literal Hebrew word here for *likeness* means an exact duplication in kind. God's plan was to create an exact duplicate of Himself. Why is this important? Because you need to understand the importance God placed on you. He didn't create you as a lowly being who has to take whatever the devil dishes out to you. He wanted you to be equal with Him. He wants you to rule on this earth the way He rules heaven.

> *It would be wrong for God to create an exact duplicate of Himself and not let him have dominion.*

God *expects* you to have dominion. It would be wrong for God to create an exact duplicate of Himself and not let him have dominion. That's why God gave Adam the authority over the earth in the Garden of Eden. God gave dominion to the creation He created and gave him a place to exercise it.

God gave Adam all the tools, all the equipment, and everything necessary to have a duplication of heaven on earth. God never intended for man to wait until he got to heaven to enjoy His goodness, experience greatness, and to live a life without limitations. It was God's intention that it would be like heaven on earth.

The moment man became a living soul he was immediately given authority. God put man in the Garden and told him to dress it and to keep it. The Hebrew text for "dress it and keep it" literally means "to guard, to protect, and to preserve from all intruders."

Guard and Protect

Adam was to guard, to protect, and to preserve his kingdom (the earth) from all intruders, but he willfully disobeyed God and knowingly allowed an intruder to enter. Adam allowed Satan into his kingdom, but God already had a master plan in place to give man back his authority in the earth.

When Jesus lived on the earth, the people were living far beneath the kind of life that God had originally planned for them. That means that they were living with limitations. They couldn't escape the sin in their lives because of what Adam did. Adam yielded his authority, but Jesus came and restored it back to man. He came to destroy the works of Satan.

Satan could not defeat Jesus while He walked on the earth. Jesus walked the earth as Adam should have walked: in dominion and authority. Jesus operated in the earth as a covenant man and willfully went to Calvary in order to strip Satan of the authority that Adam had given to him.

God laid a trap for Satan, and he walked right into it! It was a mystery "which none of the princes of this world knew: for had they known it, they would not have crucified the Lord of glory," (1 Corinthians 2:8).

The Bible says Jesus spoiled Satan, making a show of him openly (Colossians 2:15). He left Satan naked of power.

He seized him and snatched the authority from him so quickly that Satan didn't know what had happened.

After He ascended into heaven to stand before the Father victoriously, He came back to earth, appeared to His followers, and said, "All power is given unto me in heaven and in earth. Go ye therefore…" (Matthew 28:18-19). He was saying, "Now you go in My name. The Glory that has been given unto Me, I now give it to you. The authority that I have recovered from Satan now belongs to you once again."

Authority: It's Yours

Through the new birth, He has given back to you the authority that was lost in the Garden. That authority is in and on you today if you are born again. You have that same power that God once gave Adam. Religious people have a difficult time with this.

Satan will try to get you to fall for religious tradition so he can take the Word out of your heart so that you will yield your authority and become helpless. He will try to discourage you and convince you that, "There's nothing you can do." His goal is to make you think that you have no powe over him when, in all actuality, you have all the power you need over him (Luke 10:19).

For you to think that you don't have any power over the devil is a lie right out of the pit of hell. You have the dominion here; Satan is the intruder.

For you to think that you don't have any power over the devil is a lie right out of the pit of hell. You have the dominion here; Satan is the intruder. If he tries to intrude into your life whether it is in your body, your family, your finances, or your business, run him out! He's an intruder, and you are ruler over your body, your family, your finances, and your business under the lordship of Jesus Christ Who is the King of kings. The Bible says you can resist Satan and he will flee from you (James 4:7). You have authority over him! He doesn't have authority over you!

Get Wisdom

Proverbs 4:7-9 tells you how to walk in your dominion. It says, "Wisdom is the principal thing; therefore get wisdom:

.d with all thy getting get understanding. Exalt her (wisdom), and she (wisdom) shall promote thee: she shall bring thee to honour, when thou dost embrace her. She shall give to thine head an ornament of grace: a crown of glory shall she deliver to thee."

What did God say in Hosea 4:6? "My people are destroyed for lack of knowledge." A lack of knowledge will cause you to walk on the earth without your dominion. A lack of knowledge is what causes you to think God wants you poor, depressed, lonely, and sick. But when the wisdom of God (the Word of God) is the principal thing in your life, you will walk in your God-given authority. You won't allow lack, depression, and sickness to rule in your life. You will live knowing that you have all authority on earth through the Word of God to defeat Satan!

If you feel like a failure, you can learn this truth and be transformed into a winner.

If you feel like a failure, you can learn this truth and be transformed into a winner. When wisdom begins to be imparted into your heart, you can stand tall and act like a champion because you have received your authority.

There was a time in my life when I lived in defeat but not anymore. I haven't struggled with that since the day I understood the authority that Jesus has given me. Since Jesus has given you your authority once again, you can control the actions of Satan. When Satan comes around trying to tempt you, don't put up with it. Exercise your authority over him and he will flee.

Satan is under your feet! (Luke 10:19). As wisdom is imparted to you through the knowledge of God's Word and when you walk in the authority that God has given you, the devil doesn't stand a chance.

Jesus appeared to His disciples and told them, "This day all power (not some of it, not part of it, but all of it) has been given unto Me. I'm going to give it to you. Go into all the world in My name. I'm giving you the power of attorney to use My name and to exercise lordship over Satan and all of his cohorts in this earth. I'm restoring once again unto man his dominion and authority, his position as a king. I'm giving back to you the power to rule this earth. Now you go in My name and do it" (Matthew 28:18-20, author's paraphrase).

Now it's time for you to begin doing it. The early Church experienced that power and authority in the earth until Satan found out where all that power was coming from. He realized that if he could get the people to stop preaching in the name of Jesus, if he could stop the Word from coming into their hearts, then they would become helpless. Eventually that is exactly what happened.

The Church became almost powerless. Why? Because preachers began to tell everyone that the former power had passed away, that miracles had ceased, that God was not the God He used to be, and that the Holy Ghost no longer came upon men as He once did.

Satan once again was able to deceive man by religion and tradition. Jesus once said to the religious leaders of His time that they had made the commandment of God useless by their traditions (Mark 7:13). And this same thing is going on today. People are being told that God doesn't do things like He used to. They say healing and miracles have passed away, and the Church has fallen for it. When you accept things like that, you are relinquishing the authority that God has given to you and giving it back to Satan. You are giving your enemy the upper hand in a battle where the victory has already been promised to you.

Take Your Rightful Place

You need to realize that the authority, the power, and all the attributes of God Himself have been imparted to you. It's time for you to take your rightful place of authority and refuse to be defeated. Why should you be defeated when you don't have to be? It would be different if you were helpless or if circumstances were beyond your control, but they aren't. That's what the world says. The world says, "Most circumstances are beyond your control." No, they're not! That's how ordinary people talk. The problem is that the circumstances are in your control, but you have to take a stand and fight. It's your responsibility. Once again, people don't want to take responsibility. I believe that is one of the biggest problems in the world today. Everyone wants to blame someone else. If you continue to blame everyone else for your failures, you'll never succeed. You have to admit your mistakes, get in the Word, and move on. Take responsibility for your actions—or lack of them.

You have to know who you are in Christ. Once you know who you are in Christ, you will become bold. You can't walk in your authority without boldness. Speak your healing with authority. Don't be afraid to declare what God says belongs to you. It's your covenant right to do so. Exercise your dominion over Satan and run him off.

You should be just as bold as the apostles were. They weren't afraid to speak the truth, and the circumstances they faced were much worse than it is for you and me today. The disciples faced imprisonment or death, yet they still did it. How much more should we walk in our dominion?

It's Time to Reign

When Jesus stripped Satan of his authority, He put us in position where we could reign in this earth. If you don't have dominion in this earth, if you're not an heir of God and a joint-heir with Jesus, if your authority hasn't been restored to you, then what Satan did in Adam was more powerful than what God did in Jesus at Calvary. But that isn't true. The work God did in Jesus at Calvary was much greater than the work Satan did in Adam in the Garden of Eden.

As much as the devil can try to defeat you, God can increase His favor on your life and cause you to win.

God is always a step ahead of the devil. Satan doesn't even come close to being able to do what God can do. As much pressure as the devil can put on you to quit, God's grace can come upon you and enable you to stand. As much as the devil can try to defeat you, God can increase His favor on your life and cause you to win.

In other words, however big your situation is, God is bigger than that. If you've reached the point where you think you can't stand it anymore, then you've just experienced the best that Satan can do. Now get ready for God to step in and enable you to win!

The Bible says in 1 Corinthians 10:13 that Satan cannot tempt you more than you are able to bear. If you feel that you've had all you can stand and that you are about to come apart, then rejoice and say, "I have just experienced the best the devil can do so now I'm ready to experience God's grace like never before."

Don't Be Deceived

The devil is a deceiver. That is the best thing he has going for him. When you are under pressure and think you can't go any farther, then know that you have withstood Satan's best shot. You can go farther. The Bible even goes on to say in 1 Corinthians 10:13 that in your test, God will provide a way out, an escape. God is always ahead of the devil!

You Are a King

Peter tells us: "Ye also, as lively stones, are built up a spiritual house, an holy priesthood, to offer up spiritual sacrifices, acceptable to God by Jesus Christ. But ye are a chosen generation, a royal priesthood, a holy nation, a peculiar people; that ye should shew forth the praises of him who hath called you out of darkness into his marvelous light" (1 Peter 2:5, 9). Peter tells you right here that you are a king and priest.

Do you know how you become a king? There are two predominate ways: by appointment and by inheritance. David was divinely appointed as king. God sent His prophet Samuel to the house of Jesse and said, "For I have provided me a king among his sons…and thou shalt anoint unto me him whom I name unto thee" (I Samuel 16:1,3).

Samuel went down there and began to look over all of Jesse's sons. All the boys looked to Samuel like they should be king, but the Lord told him that none of them was His choice. "Do you have any more boys?" Samuel asked Jesse. "Yes, there is still the youngest. He's out tending the sheep." "Bring him in," the prophet said. So in came little David, and the Lord said to Samuel, "Arise, anoint him: for this is he" (I Samuel 16:12). David was young at the time, but God Himself appointed him king of Israel. He was divinely appointed and called by God.

2 Peter 1:3 says, "According as his divine power hath given unto us all things that pertain unto life and godliness, through the knowledge of him that hath called (divinely appointed) us to glory and virtue." You are divinely appointed; God has called you unto glory and virtue.

The second way a person becomes a king is by inheritance. After the death of the king, the crown passes to his first-born child. Jesus died, but He didn't stay dead! He became alive again to make sure that you received your rightful inheritance and to see to it that you began to reign as a king in this earth.

Don't Blame God

The Bible says you are to reign in life as a king. To reign means to rule with royal power, to exercise total authority, to dominate, and to prevail. If all believers knew this then their lives would be different. Unfortunately, people don't know who they are in Christ and what He did for them.

Ultimately, God is in control as the Judge of the earth, but He has given the dominion of it to the Body of Christ.

The world says, "If God is in control of the earth, He sure is doing a bad job of it." Ultimately, God is in control as the Judge of the earth, but He has given the dominion of it to the Body of Christ. He wants you to take your authority and reign. God didn't create the earth so He could rule over it; He created the earth so that man could rule over it. You can't blame God for the problems on this planet— blame the Christians for not exercising their God-given authority!

You were bought with a very high price. The blood of the Lamb paid for you so that you could reign in this life. Every time the devil begins to put the pressure on, many Christians back off, roll over, and play dead. Why would any child of God do that? Don't do that - don't let a defeated foe reign over you.

> *You are the one with the authority.*
> *You are the one who has supreme rule*
> *and the ability to prevail—so do it!*

If our country is in bad shape, it's because the Christians have let it get that way. It isn't God's fault; you are the one with the royal power. You are the one with the authority. You are the one who has supreme rule and the ability to prevail – so do it!

Bind the Devil

Do you know what the church has done? They've sat back and said, "Well, you never know what God is going to do. I guess this must be the will of God. After all, the Bible talks about perilous times, and here they are. There's nothing we can do about it." Oh, yes, there is! You can bind the devil in your life and decree that no weapon formed against you will prosper. You don't have to let him run all over you any more. Take charge and put him where he belongs—under your feet!

Decree Your Victory!

How do you exercise your authority and dominion? By your words! Kings call this a decree. Kings issue decrees. Did you know that you have the ability of a king to make decrees in this earth? You need to start decreeing your victory. Decree the Word over your situation. Ordinary people just keep decreeing the problem. They talk what they see—not what God says.

> *Quit telling Him about your problem and start decreeing the answer! You change your circumstances by speaking God's Word.*

If you want to live an extraordinary life, you must start decreeing the Word over your circumstances. Start decreeing the answer. God deals in solutions. He knows what's going on. Quit telling Him about your problem and start decreeing the answer! *You* change your circumstances by speaking God's Word. Give God something to work with.

The word *decree* means an official order that is settled and unchangeable. That's the way Kings operate; they issue a decree and that decree is settled and unchangeable. Their decree becomes law, and then it has to be carried out.

Do you remember when John the Baptist spoke out against King Herod and told him where he was wrong? King Herod didn't like it, so he had John thrown in prison. Then the king held a great banquet. As part of the evening's entertainment, a young woman danced for the king and his guests. Herod was so pleased with her that he called her to his side and said in front of the whole assembly: "What is it you want? Anything you want, just name it, and I'll decree it."

The young woman answered the king, "I want the head of John the Baptist on a platter." The Bible says that King Herod did not want to have John beheaded; but because of his decree, he had to do it. His royal order had to be carried out (Matthew 14:3-12).

Royal decrees are very powerful. It takes a sovereign act of God to change one. We see this in the story of Daniel in the lions' den. Daniel's enemies had persuaded King Darius to issue a decree "that whosoever shall ask a petition of any God or man for thirty days, save of thee, O king, he shall be cast into the den of lions." Daniel, of course, disobeyed this decree and continued his practice of praying three times a day to God.

His enemies lost no time in accusing him before the king, which made Darius very sad because he loved Daniel. But because of the decree, Darius had to have Daniel thrown into the lions' den. He had no choice because Daniel's enemies reminded him, "No decree or statutes which the king establisheth may be changed." It took an act of divine intervention in response to Daniel's faith to save him from the consequences of that royal decree (Daniel 6:18-22).

Aren't you ready to move from ordinary to extraordinary? If so, then start decreeing your victory.

Do you really have the ability to decree something that powerful and know that it will happen? Job 22:28 says, "Thou shalt also decree a thing, and it shall be established unto thee." It's time you start decreeing your answer and defeating the devil in your life. Aren't you ready to reign like God has given you the authority to do? Aren't you ready to move from ordinary to extraordinary? If so, then start decreeing your victory.

It's Confession Time

A lot of people get irritated about teaching on confession and say, "I'm tired of hearing about confession. I don't know why we have to watch what we say." Because that's the way kings reign! The word *confess* means "to say the same thing as; to agree with." Agree with the devil? No! Why would you do that? That's what you've been doing wrong! You've been agreeing with Satan when you should've been agreeing with God. When you talk sickness and lack, you are agreeing with the devil. He enjoys watching you live below your privileges. He is limiting what you can accomplish in life by your own words. Satan understands the system and how it operates. His best shot is keeping you in the dark and causing you to believe the way the world does.

God has already decreed His Word, and it shall not pass away. When you confess His Word, you are agreeing with a decree that has already been issued by Almighty God. When you stand in the presence of Satan and say, "By His stripes I'm healed," you are agreeing with God. Who better is there to be in partnership with? When you have decreed it, it reigns supreme and shall not pass away.

Jesus operated this way; He reigned. What did He do? He simply confessed what God's Word already said, "It is written." You don't have to go around making up new words for God. The ones He spoke are fine. You decree a thing, and it is settled and unchangeable. The Bible says, "Where the word of a king is, there is power" (Ecclesiastes. 8:4). When you begin to confess God's Word, you are agreeing with Him that what He has said has final authority.

Everybody recognizes the power and the authority of an earthly king's decree. Why should it be so hard to recognize the power and authority of a decree made by the God of the universe? His power is far greater than that of any earthly king, and He has decreed, "No weapon that is formed against thee shall prosper" (Isaiah 54:17).

Can you see why the confession of God's Word becomes more of a reality? All kings make decrees and issue official orders. You are a king so start acting like one. You are not the king of people; you are the king and master of Satan and all his allies. He is the one you are dealing with. Your warfare isn't against flesh and blood; it is against principalities and powers and dominions in this earth set up by Satan (Ephesians 6:12). You need to be issuing these decrees against him.

Tell poverty, sickness, and lack that they have no right to reign in your life. God wants you prosperous and healed. Don't let the world put boundaries on what you can accomplish. So take your God-given authority and begin to reign in life! Don't you think it' about time for you to leave the ordinary and begin to live in the extraordinary!

VIII.

Grace for Glory

Now that you understand where boundaries come from and how to get rid of them, you need to see how to keep those limitations from coming back. The devil would love to see you bound up again and thinking that the Word doesn't really work. You need to know what to do to stay free. The way to keep yourself from accepting those boundaries and those restrictions is to live in the glory.

What is the glory? A practical definition for the word *glory* is the manifested presence of God. God wants us to let His glory in our daily lives. How do we do this? By first understanding that it is our choice to let His glory into our lives.

In Exodus 33:14-15, Moses says, "And he said, My presence shall go with thee, and I will give thee rest. And he said unto him, If thy presence go not with me, carry us not up hence." In verse 18, Moses cries out to God and says, "I beseech thee, show me thy glory."

You can't fulfill what God is expecting you to do in these last days without His manifested presence.

Notice how Moses interchanges the word presence with glory. He understood that to have the glory is to be in the presence of the Almighty God. Moses said that if he couldn't expect God's glory or His presence to go with him, then he wasn't going. Why would he make a statement like that? Moses realized that without the presence of God in his life he couldn't fulfill his mission. The same is true for you. You can't fulfill what God is expecting you to do in these last days without His manifested presence.

Make the Choice

You have to choose to let God's glory in. It's a choice. It won't just come on its own. The word *let* means to permit. It's quite interesting to me that God needs our permission to manifest Himself in our midst. Why? Because He's a gentlemen. He will not force anything on us. He has given each and everyone of us a will. He won't make us let Him into our lives.

Maybe the reason you're still living with limits and haven't moved to the next level is because He hasn't been given permission to be a part of your life. Once again, God wants you to grant Him or allow Him the opportunity to manifest Himself in your midst. Why is God so interested in manifesting His presence in your midst? Because of what it will do for you. He wants you to walk in freedom. He wants you to live in the extraordinary. To live this way, you have to have His presence in your daily life. Without His presence, you will slip back into old patterns and limit yourself.

Think about the children of Israel when God called Moses to deliver them out of the land of Egypt. God wanted His people to be free. It wasn't His will that they were in bondage, just like it's not His will for you to live in bondage today. Once God told Moses to tell Pharaoh to let his people go, it became Moses' responsibility to do whatever was needed to be done for that to become reality. Likewise, you have the responsibility to do whatever is required to let His glory into your life.

God wants to manifest His presence in your home. Think about how much better your life will be, how much better you'll deal with your finances, how much better you'll deal with family issues and job issues if you get up in the morning, and before you leave your house, you have a few moments in the presence of God. That will "make your day" like nothing else ever could!

Whatever you are doing that would prevent His glory from manifesting itself in your midst, then that's what He expects you to change.

It's Your Job

Your job is to remove any hindrances or obstructions that are keeping His presence away. Whatever you are doing that would prevent His glory from manifesting itself in your midst, then that's what He expects you to change. You need to make adjustments. You may have to change your routine. If you don't have a set time to spend with God, you need to make one. His presence isn't going to fall on you out of nowhere. You have to "on purpose" plan and make time and place for Him in your life. You may already have time set aside, if so, then great. Now expect God and His glory to show up.

Matthew 5: 6 says, "Blessed are they which do hunger and thirst after righteousness: for they shall be filled." Righteousness is right standing with God. You received that when you made Jesus the Lord of your life. Another meaning of the word *righteousness* is the things that are right in the sight of God or the things that are pleasing to God.

In Matthew 6, Jesus talks about seeking first the kingdom of God and His righteousness. The Amplified Bible defines righteousness in that verse as God's way of being and doing right. If you apply that definition to Matthew 5:6, it would say, "Blessed are those who hunger and thirst for God's way of doing things and who hunger and thirst for the things that are pleasing to God."

The New American Standard reads, "Blessed are those who hunger and thirst for righteousness, for they shall be satisfied." That means that whatever you are hungry for you get. Whatever you are thirsty for you obtain. Are you hungry and thirsty after God? Do you desire more of Him in your life today?

I'm passionately pursuing more of His presence.

When you talk about hunger and thirst, you're talking about strong desire and passionate pursuit. I'm passionately pursuing more of His presence. How about you? Jesus tells us that the deepest desire of every follower of His should be for the things of God. What's your deepest desire today? If it's for something on the earth, then you need to get your priorities in order. If it's not God first, then your priorities are not in order. Seek first the kingdom of God. Being a millionaire shouldn't be your primary pursuit. You should want to know God first. Like Paul said in Philippians 3:10, "I want to know God more and to become more intimately acquainted with Him. I want to know the wonders of His person." When knowing God becomes your greatest desire, He'll bless you financially. You won't have to pursue finances. They will come to you and overtake you.

But you can't be more interested in pursuing prosperity than you are in pursuing His presence. There's nothing wrong with wanting to be prosperous. But when it is a greater desire than your desire to know Him, you have things out of order. When you hunger for an intimate relationship with the Healer, I can promise you healing comes. *God never shows up and forgets His blessings.* It's all a part of who He is. It's His character or nature.

Remember when there was such a void in your life that you knew there had to be more? You might have loved God, but deep down on the inside, there was this hole that hadn't been filled yet. Your desperation put you in a place where you made room for more. Right? Well, it doesn't stop there. Your walk with God is progressive. Every day you should strive to want more of God. God says that He will fill those that express hunger, strong desire, and passionate pursuit of Him. He says they will be satisfied.

Are You Hungry?

Experiencing the presence of God is directly linked to your hunger for it. If you are hungry for the things of God, you will obviously experience more of God than those who aren't. God isn't a respecter of persons; He is a respecter of hunger. Obviously if you crave more of God than other people do, you are going to experience more than they do.

The truth is that I got tired of being what I was over 40 years ago. I got tired of living in darkness. I got tired of just existing. I got tired of religion, and I got hungry for God. And I can tell you that God met me at the level of my hunger. Today, I'm hungrier than I've ever been in my life. How about you?

Jesus says that the things of God are to your spiritual life what food and water are to your physical life. You can't be spiritually strong without the things of God in your life just like you can't be physically strong without food and water. Have you ever seen someone who is starving? A starving person is consumed with getting food. Nothing else will satisfy that person's craving but food. Nothing else can even get that person's attention when they are starving; they're not easily distracted by anything else. They've got to have food and nothing else will satisfy.

This is the way God wants us to be about His presence. David demonstrated this when he said in Psalm 63:1, "O God, thou art my God; early will I seek thee: my soul thirsteth for thee, my flesh longeth for thee..." Notice David says, "I'm so thirsty for You my flesh yearns for You that it's like being in a dry and weary land where there is no water."

Once you've been in His presence,
then you'll want more—
He'll give you more.

God is saying to us that if we will just show Him that we are hungry and thirsty for Him, then He will fill us. He will satisfy us. Everything we truly desire, truly want, and everything that will truly make us happy is in His presence." Only God can satisfy your cravings. Only He can fulfill your greatest desires and make you happy. He's not hiding from you. He wants to be close to you. Nothing else can satisfy like being near Him. Once you've been in His presence, then you'll want more—He'll give you more.

God Always Responds

Psalm 107:9 (NAS) says, *"For he has satisfied the thirsty soul and the hungry soul he has filled with what is good."* God always responds to hunger. All He wants is to be first place in your life. Every time you go to God with a hungry heart, He will manifest Himself to you.

Higher Things

Colossians 3:2 says, "Set your affection on things above not on things on the earth." The Amplified Bible says it this way, "Set your affection on the higher things." You might be thinking, "If I get that serious about God, what about my career? What about what I want to do in life?" Well, the Bible says that if you will delight yourself in the Lord, He will give you the desires of your heart (Psalm 37:4). "But I won't have a life if I give it all to God." That's not true. He will provide for you a better life than you've ever imagined.

You want the best for your kids and so does God. Sometimes to give your children what is best for them, you have to do something they may not want to do, but in the long run, it puts them on the path to success. They don't like doing homework, but if they don't, they won't succeed in school.

It's the same with God. He does the same thing with His children. You may not like some of the steps, that He requires you to take, but He sees the master plan, you don't. His vision for you is greater than what you can imagine, and He is trying to put you on the right track.

Stop Siding With the Devil

You might be thinking, "Well, Jerry, it would be much easier to dive into this if I didn't have so much pressure on me right now. You don't understand. I have all these financial demands and burdens. I want to get into this, I want to experience more of God's presence, but all these things are going on around me and pulling me down."

You're thinking, "I can't be spending all day listening to God." Why not? You spend all day listening to the devil when you worry.

Are you saying that when the conditions are perfect, then you'll get your act together? Since when have you known a day in your life when all the conditions were perfect? All you're doing is siding with the devil. You're thinking, "I can't be spending all day listening to God." Why not? You spend all day listening to the devil when you worry. Worrying is listening to the devil. You're giving Satan first place.

Worry is just another limitation
Satan uses to keep you defeated.

Worry is just another limitation Satan uses to keep you defeated. How is it that you can worry all day and yet still work? Why can't you think on what God says while you're working? What about on your break? Instead of getting another cup of coffee, why don't you have a praise break? Go find a place where you can shout a little bit and get those negative thoughts out of your mind.

Those that seek the Lord shall not want any good thing. Do you honestly think that getting extremely serious with God and hungering for His presence like never before is going to deprive you of something? No, it's going to open doors in your life like you have never walked through before. It's going to open blessings in your life that you have never experienced before. But the priority has got to be pursuing Him. You have to pursue His presence if you want His best.

Just think how much better your life would be, what better decisions you would make in life if you experienced His presence on a daily basis.

It's Up to You

You have a choice. You have to choose to let His glory into your life. He's asking you to take the responsibility for allowing this to happen. God wants His manifested presence in your home. Just think how much better your life would be, what better decisions you would make in life if you experienced His presence on a daily basis. What would that do to your business? What would that do to your finances if you experienced the manifested presence of God on a daily basis?

Take the First Step

James 4:8 says, "Draw nigh to God, and he will draw nigh to you." That certainly destroys the mindset of "I'm just waiting on God" because it is quite obvious He's waiting on you. You can be just as close to God as you want to be. In other words, you take the first step. I call that the law of reciprocation. God reacts to your action. You take a step toward Him and He says, "I'll respond to that and I'll take a step toward you."

In the Amplified Bible, James 4:8 says, "Come close to God, and He will come close to you." I hear people all the time praying, "Oh Lord, I just want to be close to You." Well, take a step then. But the mindset is "I'm just waiting on God," when in reality, He's just waiting on us.

The Psalmist said, I have tasted God and He is good (Psalm 34:8). When you taste something that is good then you want more of it. I've been in His presence. I've experienced the glory of God in my life, and I want more.

If you want to live life in the extraordinary, then you need a sense of urgency toward pursuing the presence of God.

If you want to live life in the extraordinary, then you need a sense of urgency toward pursuing the presence of God. When Moses said, "Show me thy glory," in Exodus 33:18, he was expressing a sense of urgency. He needed it more than he needed anything else. How desperate are you for the presence of God? How desperate are you for change in your life? Moses knew he could not accomplish the assignment God had given him without God's presence in his life.

It's a Relationship

Your Christianity would be so dull if you never experienced the presence of God. That's the reason so many people walk away from it because all they ever experience is religion. Christianity was never meant to be a religion, it's a relationship. You are in partnership with God – you're in

His family. If you're in a relationship with God, then don't you think that He would like to show up every once in a while? Don't you want your business partner to show up every once in a while? How about your spouse? It's the same with God. He wants to show up in your life.

The World Needs Undeniable Proof

Moses reached a point in His life where he said that he couldn't go any farther without the presence of God. When you get to the place in your life where you feel like you cannot go any farther without the presence of God, then you'll understand Moses' urgency for a manifestation of His presence. Moses knew that he couldn't accomplish his mission without it. Likewise, you cannot accomplish your mission today in this dark world without the manifestations of the presence of God in your personal life. The world needs to see undeniable proof of a resurrected Savior – in you!

After Jesus was raised from the dead, He showed Himself alive by many infallible proofs (Acts 1:3). He then took His position at the right hand of God, and as the early disciples and apostles went out preaching, they experienced His manifested presence with many signs and wonders (Acts 5:12 and 14:3). Why? Because the apostles needed more than just the right message to preach. They needed manifestations of the One about whom they were preaching. Our world today is dark, corrupt, immoral, and carnal-minded, and it's going to take more than just the right message to reach them. It's going to take infallible proofs and manifestations of the living Savior.

Mark 16:20 says that the disciples went everywhere preaching the Gospel. The Lord was working with them confirming the Word with signs following. God wants His word to be confirmed in your life as well.

His Presence = His Goodness

When Moses said to God, "Show me thy glory," God said back to him, "I will make all my goodness pass before thee." (Exodus 33:19) Notice that Moses didn't say anything about wanting to see God's goodness. He said he wanted to see His glory. In the mind of God, you can't have His presence without His goodness. They go hand in hand.

Maybe you have been asking God for prosperity, success, healing, and deliverance and that's fine, but if you will pursue His presence more than those things, then you'll receive all of those things in addition to His presence. His goodness always comes with His presence.

Some additional words that are synonymous with the glory of the Lord are: the splendor, the magnificence, the majesty, and the beauty of God. Think about these words. When Moses said, "Show me your glory," he was saying, "Show me Your splendor. Show me Your magnificence. Show me Your majesty. Show me Your beauty."

Now, if you get in the presence of the beauty, the majesty, the magnificence, and the splendor of God, do you think for one moment that any demon would be able to stand against you? Would any sickness be able to stand? Would any assignment of the adversary be able to stand? No, not in the presence of the magnificence, the beauty, and the splendor of God.

When you ask God, "Show me your glory," you're asking for something huge. You're asking for something big, and God is committed to showing you if you show Him you're truly hungry for it.

True Worship

The presence of God manifesting in your life is directly linked to true worship. Jesus is looking for true worshippers today. In 2 Chronicles 5:13, it says, "It came even to pass, as the trumpeters and singers were as one, to make one sound to be heard in praising and thanking the LORD; and when they lifted up their voice with the trumpets and cymbals and instruments of music, and praised the LORD, saying, For he is good…"

The presence of God manifesting in your life is directly linked to true worship.

True praise and worship has to do with you expressing to God how good He is. Apparently God enjoys hearing His people tell Him, "You have been good to me. You're a good God."

God is good, and His mercy endures forever. True praise and worship not only has to do with you expressing to God how good He's been to you, but also expressing to Him how deeply grateful you are for His mercy. Thank God for His mercy. If it wasn't for His mercy, we would all be on our way to hell.

If it wasn't for His mercy, we would know nothing about the abundant life. How often do we thank God for His mercy? This is connected to worship.

It goes on to say in 2 Chronicles 5:14, "For he is good; for his mercy endureth for ever: that then the house was filled with a cloud, even the house of the LORD; So that the priests could not stand to minister by reason of the cloud: for the glory of the LORD had filled the house of God."

The presence of the Lord was so strong that the priests couldn't minister. When was the last time you saw His presence like that? Psalm 18:3, "I will call upon the Lord who is worthy to be praised and so shall I be saved from my enemies." Notice how praise came first, and then the deliverance from his enemies followed. Praise always stops the adversary from accomplishing what he set out to do.

A Secret Place

Exodus 25 talks about making a sanctuary so God can dwell among the people. You need to develop a special place that belongs to you. A place where you can get alone with God and hear from Him. He promises that He will meet with you in that secret place.

The Bible tells us that God inhabits the praises of His people. That means He will set up His throne in the midst of your praise. David's praise caused God to set up His throne right there where David was and that's why his enemy had to turn back.

When you praise Him, He will set up His throne in the midst of your praise, and He will exercise His authority as Judge of the universe.

Think about what happens when you enter a courtroom. When you first go in, you sit down. There may be a lot of people talking, but the moment the judge comes through that door, everyone becomes silent and rises from their seats. The moment the judge sits down behind his desk everybody knows that he's about to exercise his authority as judge. And that is exactly what God is telling us He will do for us. He inhabits the praises of His people. When you praise Him, He will set up His throne in the midst of your praise, and He will exercise His authority as Judge of the universe. He promises that your enemy will turn back and justice shall be served.

Justice Will be Served

What is justice when you're sick? Healing. What is justice when you're broke? Prosperity. What is justice when the devil has you in bandage? Deliverance. That's justice in the mind of God. And you can have it if you pursue His presence. His presence first, then everything else you need will follow.

You've seen that God inhabits the praise of His people. That means when you praise and worship the Lord, He's going to show up in your situation. There's no demon from hell that will be able to hold you back or keep you down.

So practice pursuing His presence and just watch how drastically your life will change. You'll soon see that you will have no limits and you'll have no boundaries. You'll no longer live in the realm of the ordinary but in the realm of the extraordinary.

Prayer of Salvation

If you were to die today, where would you spend eternity?
If you have accepted Jesus Christ as your Lord and Savior,
you can be assured that when you die, you will go directly
into the presence of God in Heaven. If you have not accepted Jesus as your personal Lord and Savior, is there
any reason why you can't make Jesus the Lord of your life
right now? Please pray this prayer out loud, and as you do,
pray with a sincere and trusting heart and you will be born
again.

Dear God in Heaven,

I come to you in the Name of Jesus to receive salvation
and eternal life. I believe that Jesus is Your Son. I believe
that He died on the cross for my sins, and that you raised
him from the dead. I receive Jesus now into my life. Jesus,
come into my heart. I welcome you as my Lord and Savior.
I confess with my mouth that I am saved and born again. I
am now a child of God.

Amen.

Dr. Jerry Savelle was an average, blue-collar man who was struggling and needed God's help. While he considered himself a "nobody," when he became a believer God told him not to worry about it because He was a master at making champions out of nobodies. God has since taken Dr. Savelle from being a constant quitter to a man who knows how to stand on the Word of God until victory is experienced. Because of the life-changing combination of God's faithfulness and Dr. Savelle's "no quit" attitude, his life is totally different than it was thirty-eight years ago.

Since 1969, Dr. Savelle has been traveling the world teaching people how to win in life. Dr. Savelle has ministered in more than three thousand churches in twenty six nations, and has overseas offices in the United Kingdom, Australia, Canada, and a mission's outreach in Tanzania.

God has used Dr. Savelle to impact people who are burned out on religion and who have backslidden in their walk with God, as well as Christians who have a need to hear the Word of God presented in terms applicable to their lives, dreams, and destinies. He is the host of the Jerry

Savelle Ministries television broadcast which airs in two hundred countries worldwide.

Dr. Savelle is the author of more than forty books, including his bestsellers, *If Satan Can't Steal Your Joy, He Can't Keep Your Goods* and *Called to Battle, Destined To Win.* He and his wife, Carolyn, also serve as founding Pastors of Heritage of Faith Christian Center in Crowley, Texas.

Other Books by Jerry Savelle

Called To Battle, Destined To Win
Living In The Fullness Of The Blessing
Increase God's Way
Receive God's Best
Free to be Yourself
The God of the Breakthrough Will Visit Your House
If Satan Can't Steal Your Dreams, He Can't Control Your
Destiny
Free at Last from Oppression
Free at Last from Old Habits
Thoughts – The Battle between Your Ears
Expect the Extraordinary
In the Footsteps of a Prophet
The Last Frontier
Take Charge of Your Financial Destiny
From Devastation to Restoration
Turning Your Adversity into Victory
Honoring Your Heritage of Faith
Don't Let Go of Your Dreams
Faith Building Daily Devotionals
The Force of Joy
If Satan Can't Steal Your Joy, He Can't Keep Your Goods
A Right Mental Attitude
The Nature of Faith
Sharing Jesus Effectively
How to Overcome Financial Famine
You're Somebody Special to God
The Established Heart

Further Resources

For additional products, including book, audios and
videos, visit the Jerry Savelle Ministries website at:

www.jerrysavelle.org

USA OFFICE
P.O. Box 748
Crowley, TX 76036
Phone: 817-297-3155

AUSTRALIA OFFICE
Locked Bag 2,
Burleigh BC, QLD, 4220
Phone: 61 7 5526-6522

CANADA OFFICE
P.O. Box 7000
London, Ontario
N6P 1W4
Phone: 519-652-1611

EUROPE OFFICE
11 Welsh St.
Chepstow
NP16 5LN
Phone: 44(0) 1291 628071

p.2 - Revelation - 60 Vision - 77 % 82 Increase by